# Amigurumi at Home

## CROCHET PLAYFUL PILLOWS, RUGS, BASKETS, AND MORE

ANA PAULA RÍMOLI

Martingale®
*Create with Confidence*

Amigurumi at Home:
Crochet Playful Pillows, Rugs, Baskets, and More
© 2014 by Ana Paula Rímoli

Martingale®
Create with Confidence

Martingale®
19021 120th Ave. NE, Ste. 102
Bothell, WA 98011-9511 USA
ShopMartingale.com

Printed in China
19 18 17 16 15 14          8 7 6 5 4 3 2 1

Library of Congress Cataloging-in-Publication Data is available upon request.

ISBN: 978-1-60468-432-2

MISSION STATEMENT
Dedicated to providing quality products and service to inspire creativity.

CREDITS

**PRESIDENT AND CEO**: Tom Wierzbicki

**EDITOR IN CHIEF**: Mary V. Green

**DESIGN DIRECTOR**: Paula Schlosser

**MANAGING EDITOR**: Karen Costello Soltys

**ACQUISITIONS EDITOR**: Karen M. Burns

**TECHNICAL EDITOR**: Ursula Reikes

**COPY EDITOR**: Tiffany Mottet

**PRODUCTION MANAGER**: Regina Girard

**COVER AND INTERIOR DESIGNER**: Adrienne Smitke

**PHOTOGRAPHER**: Brent Kane

**ILLUSTRATOR**: Kathryn Conway

# Dedication

*Para Oli y Marti, las quiero hasta el cielo!*

# Contents

# Introduction

Here I am, writing an introduction for a book again, and it still seems very unreal . . . . When I wrote the intro for my first book, *Amigurumi World,* back in 2007, Marti (now almost seven years old) was a little baby, and Oli (now ten!) was only four years old. Time passes by so fast. This "crocheting adventure" started because of them, and it continues to be for and inspired by them.

After years and years (10, to be exact!) of saying that she would live with us forever, and making plans to redo the attic, Oli told me a couple of months ago that she might "rent an apartment" in New York City some day. Now imagine my face—eyes wide open, not knowing if I should cry or lock her up! What do you mean rent an apartment? So she's planning to leave me? *What?* I knew it would eventually happen, but does she have to change her mind that fast? Really?

So with that in mind, I figured I have to crochet new stuff to hide cameras in (I doubt she'll take stuffed toys with her), and the idea for this book was born! She *will* need a cute little rug, and some pillows. Okay, not really. (I'm not that crazy!) But as the girls grow up and their stuffed toys move to the attic (since Oli won't be living there with her family anymore, there will be plenty of space), I feel like they're going to need other stuff to make their spaces their own, and to be reminded of the person who loves them the most in the whole universe.

This book is filled with fun accessories for your home, to make it cuter and to bring out smiles. What's better than that? I hope you love it and find the perfect projects for every special person you know, including yourself.

Thank you very much for choosing this book. Happy crocheting!

~ *Ana*

# Owl Pillow

*Owls are supposed to be super smart (at least they look it), so we should always have one around. Pick your owl's colors to match your decor and listen to what he or she has to say.*

**FINISHED SIZE: APPROX 9½" WIDE x 12" TALL**

## MATERIALS

Worsted-weight yarn in tan (approx 92 yds), and scraps of brown, white, dark green, light green, orange, purple, and sky blue (approx 22 yds of each)

Size J-10 (6 mm) crochet hook

Black craft felt for eyes

Sewing thread and sharp needle

Tapestry needle

Fiberfill or stuffing of your choice

Optional: 2 star buttons, approx ½" diameter

## SPECIAL STITCH

**Double crochet cluster (dc cluster):** Yarn over hook and insert hook into next st, yarn over hook and pull through st, yarn over hook and pull through 2 loops on hook, (yarn over hook and insert hook into same st, yarn over hook and pull through st, yarn over hook and pull through 2 loops) twice, yarn over hook and pull through all 4 loops on hook. One dc cluster made.

## EYE ROUNDIES

Each eye is made of three crocheted circles, with a felt circle sewn in the middle.

### Outer Eye

Make 2.

**Rnd 1:** Using brown yarn, ch 2, 5 sc in second ch from hook.

**Rnd 2:** Sc 2 in every sc around. (10 sts)

**Rnd 3:** *Sc 1, 2 sc in next sc*, rep 5 times. (15 sts)

**Rnd 4:** *Sc 2, 2 sc in next sc*, rep 5 times. (20 sts)

**Rnd 5:** *Sc 3, 2 sc in next sc*, rep 5 times. (25 sts)

**Rnd 6:** *Sc 4, 2 sc in next sc*, rep 5 times. (30 sts)

**Rnd 7:** *Sc 5, 2 sc in next sc*, rep 5 times. (35 sts)

**Rnd 8:** Sc 35.

Sl st 1 and fasten off, leaving long tail for sewing. Set aside.

## Middle Eye

Make 2.

Using white yarn, rep rnds 1–5 of outer roundie.

**Rnd 6:** Sc 25.

Sl st 1 and fasten off, leaving long tail for sewing. Set aside.

## Inner Eye

Make 2.

Using dark-green yarn, rep rnds 1–4 of outer roundie.

Sl st 1 and fasten off, leaving long tail for sewing.

Cut eyes from black felt (patt on page 11). Use sewing thread and sharp needle to sew eye to middle of dark-green roundie. Use yarn and tapestry needle to sew dark-green roundie to white roundie, and then sew both to brown roundie. Set aside.

## BODY

Using tan yarn, loosely ch 31.

**Rnd 1:** Sc 30 starting in second bump at back of ch (see page 72), then work 30 sc on opposite side of ch (front loops of ch). (60 sts)

**Rnds 2–26:** Sc 60.

**Rnd 27:** Sc 45. Work only 45 sts so color changes will be in back of owl.

**Work on face:** Sew complete eye units in place, use tapestry needle to embroider beak with orange yarn.

Change to brown yarn.

**Rnd 28:** Work 60 dc clusters around.

**Rnd 29:** Sc 60.

**Rnds 30 and 31:** Rep rnds 28 and 29 with purple yarn.

**Rnds 32 and 33:** Rep rnds 28 and 29 with light-green yarn.

**Rnds 34 and 35:** Rep rnds 28 and 29 with sky-blue yarn.

**Rnds 36–41:** Rep rnds 30–35.

**Rnds 42 and 43:** Rep rnds 28 and 29 with brown.

**Rnds 44 and 45:** Rep rnds 28 and 29 with orange.

**Rnd 46:** Sc 60 with orange.

Sl st 1 and fasten off, leaving long tail for sewing. Stuff owl and sew open end closed.

## EAR

Make 2.

**Rnd 1:** Using tan yarn, ch 2, 5 sc in second ch from hook.

**Rnd 2:** Sc 5.

**Rnd 3:** Sc 2 in every sc around. (10 sts)

**Rnd 4:** Sc 10.

Sl st 1 and fasten off, leaving long tail for sewing. Sew ears to top corners of head.

## WING

Make 2.

**Rnd 1:** Using tan yarn, ch 2, 5 sc in second ch from hook.

**Rnd 2:** Sc 5.

**Rnd 3:** Sc 2 in every sc around. (10 sts)

**Rnd 4:** Sc 10.

**Rnd 5:** *Sc 1, 2 sc in next sc*, rep 5 times. (15 sts)

**Rnd 6:** Sc 15.

**Rnd 7:** *Sc 2, 2 sc in next sc*, rep 5 times. (20 sts)

**Rnds 8–12:** Sc 20.

**Rnd 13:** *Sc 2, dec 1*, rep 5 times. (15 sts)

**Rnd 14:** Sc 15.

**Rnd 15:** *Sc 1, dec 1*, rep 5 times. (10 sts)

**Rnd 16:** Sc 10.

Sl st 1 and fasten off, leaving long tail for sewing. Sew open end tog and sew wings to side of body on tan rnd just above brown rnd on each side.

**Owl eye**

*Back of pillow*

# House Pillow

*We just came back from a week of vacation at the beach and had the best time! We wanted to stay there forever, but we also wanted to get back to our place. Isn't it the best feeling when you actually open the door and you're home? This little pillow is a reminder of how lucky we are to have a smiling home and family to always come back to.*

**FINISHED SIZE: APPROX 10" WIDE x 13" TALL**

## MATERIALS

Worsted-weight yarn in tan (approx 98 yds), blue (approx 92 yds), and small amounts of purple, orange, and white (approx 22 yds of each)

Size J-10 (6 mm) crochet hook

Black craft felt for eyes and smile

Sewing thread and sharp needle

Tapestry needle

Fiberfill or stuffing of your choice

## HOUSE

Start crocheting at top of house.

**Rnd 1:** Using blue yarn, ch 2, 6 sc in second ch from hook.

**Rnd 2:** Sc 2 in every sc around. (12 sts)

**Rnd 3:** Sc 12.

**Rnd 4:** *Sc 1, 2 sc in next sc*, rep 6 times. (18 sts)

**Rnd 5:** Sc 18.

**Rnd 6:** *Sc 2, 2 sc in next sc*, rep 6 times. (24 sts)

**Rnd 7:** Sc 24.

**Rnd 8:** *Sc 3, 2 sc in next sc*, rep 6 times. (30 sts)

**Rnd 9:** Sc 30.

**Rnd 10:** *Sc 4, 2 sc in next sc*, rep 6 times. (36 sts)

**Rnd 11:** Sc 36.

**Rnd 12:** *Sc 5, 2 sc in next sc*, rep 6 times. (42 sts)

**Rnd 13:** Sc 42.

**Rnd 14:** *Sc 6, 2 sc in next sc*, rep 6 times. (48 sts)

**Rnd 15:** Sc 48.

**Rnd 16:** *Sc 7, 2 sc in next sc*, rep 6 times. (54 sts)

**Rnd 17:** Sc 54.

**Rnd 18:** *Sc 8, 2 sc in next sc*, rep 6 times. (60 sts)

**Rnd 19:** Sc 60.

**Rnd 20:** *Sc 9, 2 sc in next sc*, rep 6 times. (66 sts)

**Rnd 21:** Sc 66.

**Rnd 22:** *Sc 10, 2 sc in next sc*, rep 6 times. (72 sts)

**Rnd 23:** Sc 72.

**Rnd 24:** *Sc 11, 2 sc in next sc*, rep 6 times. (78 sts)

**Rnds 25–35:** Sc 78.

Change to tan yarn.

**Rnd 36:** Sc 78 through back loops only (see page 72). (You'll use front loops later when making the wavy edge along bottom of roof.)

**Rnds 37–45:** Sc 78.

**Rnd 46:** To make pocket opening, 13 sc, ch 13, sk 13 sts, 52 sc.

**Rnd 47:** Sc 13, 13 sc in 13-st ch, 52 sc. (78 sts)

**Rnds 48–64:** Sc 78.

Sl st 1 and fasten off, leaving long tail for sewing.

## POCKET INSERT

Using blue yarn, loosely ch 17, turn.

**Row 1:** Sc 16 starting in second ch from hook, turn.

**Rows 2–21:** Ch 1, 16 sc, turn.

Fasten off, leaving long tail for sewing.

Turn pillow inside out, and align pocket piece with opening you left in rnd 46. Use yarn and tapestry needle to sew all around perimeter.

## WAVY EDGE

The wavy edge makes the bottom part of the roof. Starting at back of house, join blue yarn in 1 of front loops you left in rnd 36.

**Row 1:** Sc 78.

**Row 2:** *Dc 4 in next sc, sk 1 sc, sl st 1*, rep around.

Fasten off.

## LITTLE FLAG

Make 5.

Using purple yarn, loosely ch 5, turn.

**Row 1:** Sc 4 starting in second ch from hook, turn.

**Rows 2 and 3:** Ch 1, 4 sc, turn.

Fasten off, leaving long tail for sewing.

Using orange yarn, embroider line on roof approx 16" long for little flags to hang from, starting at left side of house just above wavy edge, and curving around to top of roof and around back (see photos on pages 12 and 15). Using purple yarn and tapestry needle, sew flags along embroidered line. Embroider a spot of color on some flags if desired.

## BIG WINDOW AND DOOR

Make 1 of each.

Using white yarn for window, or orange yarn for door, loosely ch 11.

**Row 1:** Sc 10 starting in second ch from hook, turn.

**Rows 2–9:** Ch 1, 10 sc, turn.

Fasten off, leaving long tail for sewing.

Using purple yarn and referring to photo on page 12, embroider a line ¼" from edge all around window and door. Add a line of orange yarn below purple line on big window.

## SMALL WINDOW

Using white yarn, loosely ch 7.

**Row 1:** Sc 6 starting in second ch from hook, turn.

**Rows 2–9:** Ch 1, 6 sc, turn.

Fasten off, leaving long tail for sewing.

Embroider around small window as for big window.

## FINISHING

Cut eyes and smile from black felt (patts below right). Using sewing thread and sharp needle, sew eyes to windows and smile to door. Using yarn and tapestry needle, sew windows and door in place referring to photo on page 12. Stuff house and sew open end closed.

*Put special treasures in the little pocket.*

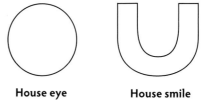

**House eye**          **House smile**

# Robot Pajama Holder

*Martina has already called this one, so when I get it back from the publisher—after all the pattern editing, reviewing, and picture taking is finished, which it will be by the time you read this—it's going on Marti's bed! I think it'll look really cute there, and on your kid's bed too.*

**FINISHED SIZE: APPROX 13½" WIDE x 24½" TALL**

## MATERIALS

Worsted-weight yarn in light blue (approx 98 yds), medium blue (approx 278 yds), dark blue (approx 98 yds), and yellow (approx 88 yds)

Size J-10 (6 mm) crochet hook

Black, white, and red craft felt for clock face, eyes, heart, and smile

Sewing thread and sharp needle

Tapestry needle

Fiberfill or stuffing of your choice

Two buttons, approx 1" diameter

## HEAD

Using medium-blue yarn, loosely ch 61.

**Rnd 1:** Sc 60 starting in second bump at back of ch (see page 72), then work 60 sc on opposite side of ch (front loops of ch). (120 sts)

**Rnds 2–51:** Sc 120.

**Work on face:** Cut eye circles from black and white felt, and smile from black felt (patts on page 20). Using sewing thread and sharp needle, sew small white circle to black circle, then sew both to large white circle. Sew eyes and smile in place.

Sl st 1 and fasten off, leaving long tail for sewing. Stuff head and use tapestry needle to sew open end closed.

## EARS

Make 2.

**Rnd 1:** Using yellow yarn, ch 2, 6 sc in second ch from hook.

**Rnd 2:** Sc 2 in every sc around. (12 sts)

**Rnd 3:** *Sc 1, 2 sc in next sc*, rep 6 times. (18 sts)

**Rnd 4:** *Sc 2, 2 sc in next sc*, rep 6 times. (24 sts)

**Rnd 5:** *Sc 3, 2 sc in next sc*, rep 6 times. (30 sts)

**Rnds 6–11:** Sc 30.

Sl st 1 and fasten off, leaving long tail for sewing. Stuff and sew ears to sides of head starting about 1" from top on each side.

**BODY PILLOW OPTION**

*To make a body pillow instead of a pajama holder, omit the pocket opening from round 47 and just single crochet all 80 stitches in the round.*

## BODY

Using medium-blue yarn, loosely ch 41.

**Rnd 1:** Sc 40 starting in second bump at back of ch, then work 40 sc on opposite side of ch (front loops of ch). (80 sts)

**Rnds 2–13:** Sc 80.

**Rnds 14–23:** Sc 80 with light-blue yarn.

**Rnds 24–28:** Sc 80 with dark-blue yarn.

**Rnds 29–36:** Sc 80 with medium-blue yarn.

**Rnds 37–46:** Sc 80 with dark-blue yarn.

**Rnd 47:** To make pocket opening, 5 sc, ch 30, sk 30 sts, 45 sc.

**Rnd 48:** Sc 5, 30 sc in ch-30 sp, 45 sc. (80 sts)

**Rnds 49 and 50:** Sc 80.

**Rnds 51–56:** Sc 80 with medium-blue yarn.

Fasten off, leaving long tail for sewing. Sew open end tog and sew to bottom of head.

## POCKET FLAP FOR PAJAMA HOLDER

Holding robot with head down, join yarn to sc sts to right of opening you left in rnd 48. Make sure to join yarn in opening closer to head, so flap will close down once robot is turned right side up.

**Rows 1–4:** Ch 1, 30 sc, turn.

**Row 5:** Dec 1, 26 sc, dec 1, turn. (28 sts)

Make buttonholes.

**Row 6:** Dec 1, 1 sc, ch 2, sk 2 sts, 18 sc, ch 2, sk 2 sts, 1 sc, dec 1. (26 sts)

**Row 7:** Ch 1, 2 sc, 2 sc in ch-2 sp, 18 sc, 2 sc in ch-2 sp, 2 sc.

Fasten off.

## ARM

Make 2.

Using dark-blue yarn, loosely ch 11.

**Rnd 1:** Sc 10 starting in second bump at back of ch, then work 10 sc on opposite side of ch (front loops of ch). (20 sts)

**Rnds 2–13:** Sc 20.

**Rnds 14–16:** Sc 20 with yellow yarn.

**Rnds 17–20:** Sc 20 with medium-blue yarn.

**Rnds 21–23:** Sc 20 with yellow yarn.

Sl st 1 and fasten off, leaving long tail for sewing. Stuff a little, sew open end closed, and sew arms to each side of body front below neck at slight angle.

## LEG

Make 2.

Using yellow yarn, loosely ch 11.

**Rnd 1:** Sc 10 starting in second bump at back of ch, then work 10 sc on opposite side of ch (front loops of ch). (20 sts)

**Rnds 2–6:** Sc 20.

**Rnds 7–23:** Sc 20 with dark-blue yarn.

Sl st 1 and fasten off, leaving long tail for sewing. Stuff a little, sew open end tog, and sew legs to each side of body front starting about 1" from bottom.

## BELLY CLOCK

Belly clock is made in two parts.

### Outer Circle

**Rnd 1:** Using yellow yarn, ch 2, 5 sc in second ch from hook.

**Rnd 2:** Sc 2 in every sc around. (10 sts)

**Rnd 3:** *Sc 1, 2 sc in next sc*, rep 5 times. (15 sts)

**Rnd 4:** *Sc 2, 2 sc in next sc*, rep 5 times. (20 sts)

**Rnd 5:** *Sc 3, 2 sc in next sc*, rep 5 times. (25 sts)

**Rnd 6:** *Sc 4, 2 sc in next sc*, rep 5 times. (30 sts)

**Rnd 7:** *Sc 5, 2 sc in next sc*, rep 5 times. (35 sts)

**Rnd 8:** *Sc 6, 2 sc in next sc*, rep 5 times. (40 sts)

**Rnd 9:** Sc 40.

Sl st 1 and fasten off, leaving long tail for sewing. Set aside.

### Inner Circle

Using light-blue yarn, rep rnds 1–6 of outer circle.

**Rnd 7:** Sc 30.

Sl st 1 and fasten off, leaving long tail for sewing.

## FINISHING

**Clock face:** Cut hands from black felt (patts on page 20), and use sewing thread and sharp needle to sew in place on inner circle.

Using yarn and tapestry needle, sew inner circle on top of outer circle, then sew both on robot's belly.

**Heart:** Cut heart from red felt (patt on page 20). Using sewing thread and sharp needle, sew heart next to clock, about three quarters of the way around, stuff a little, and finish sewing.

**Pocket flap:** Sew buttons just below pocket opening to correspond with buttonholes.

*Store your pajamas in the pocket.*

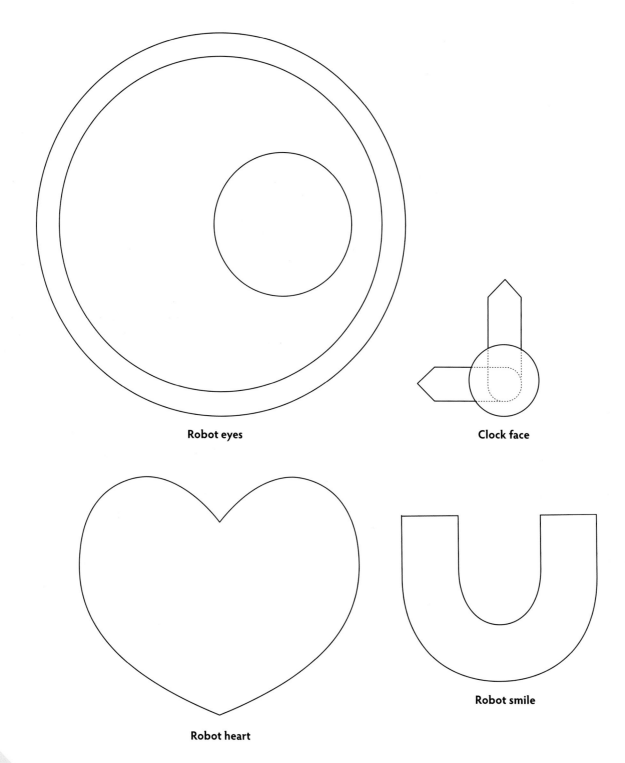

Robot eyes

Clock face

Robot heart

Robot smile

*amigurumi at home*

# Dog and Cat Foot Warmers

*Our little dogs, Santiago and Federico, are not allowed upstairs (Oli's allergic to cats and other stuff, so we try to minimize shedding where she sleeps), but I've always thought it'd be amazingly comforting to have one of them sleep on my feet in the winter. There's no way my husband would let them on our bed though! So I made these for the end of the girls' beds—it will NOT be the same at all, but at least their feet will be extra warm. Plus, Marti pointed out that they'll also be great to have in her lap while she's reading on the couch.*

⬆ **FINISHED SIZE: DOG: APPROX 11" WIDE x 20" LONG, CAT: APPROX 11" WIDE x 18" LONG**

## MATERIALS

**Dog:** Worsted-weight yarn in tan (approx 278 yds), plus light blue, medium blue, orange, and white (approx 186 yds of each)

**Cat:** Worsted-weight yarn in white (approx 278 yds), plus light pink, medium pink, and green (approx 186 yds of each)

### For both:

Size J-10 (6 mm) crochet hook

12 mm plastic eyes with safety backings

Black embroidery floss and embroidery needle

Tapestry needle

Fiberfill or stuffing of your choice

## DOG MUZZLE

**Rnd 1:** Using white yarn, ch 2, 5 sc in second ch from hook.

**Rnd 2:** Sc 2 in every sc around. (10 sts)

**Rnd 3:** *Sc 1, 2 sc in next sc*, rep 5 times. (15 sts)

**Rnd 4:** *Sc 2, 2 sc in next sc*, rep 5 times. (20 sts)

**Rnds 5 and 6:** Sc 20.

Sl st 1 and fasten off, leaving long tail for sewing. Embroider nose and smile. Set aside.

## DOG EYE ROUNDIE

**Rnd 1:** Using white yarn, ch 2, 5 sc in second ch from hook.

**Rnd 2:** Sc 2 in every sc around. (10 sts)

**Rnd 3:** *Sc 1, 2 sc in next sc*, rep 5 times. (15 sts)

**Rnd 4:** *Sc 2, 2 sc in next sc*, rep 5 times. (20 sts)

Sl st 1 and fasten off, leaving long tail for sewing. Set aside.

## CAT MUZZLE

**Rnd 1:** Using white yarn, ch 2, 5 sc in second ch from hook.

**Rnd 2:** Sc 2 in every sc around. (10 sts)

**Rnd 3:** *Sc 1, 2 sc in next sc*, rep 5 times. (15 sts)

**Rnd 4:** Sc 15.

Sl st 1 and fasten off, leaving long tail for sewing. Embroider nose and smile. Set aside.

## DOG AND CAT HEAD

**Rnd 1:** Using tan yarn for dog or white yarn for cat, ch 2, 6 sc in second ch from hook.

**Rnd 2:** Sc 2 in every sc around. (12 sts)

**Rnd 3:** *Sc 1, 2 sc in next sc*, rep 6 times. (18 sts)

**Rnd 4:** *Sc 2, 2 sc in next sc*, rep 6 times. (24 sts)

**Rnd 5:** *Sc 3, 2 sc in next sc*, rep 6 times. (30 sts)

**Rnd 6:** *Sc 4, 2 sc in next sc*, rep 6 times. (36 sts)

**Rnd 7:** *Sc 5, 2 sc in next sc*, rep 6 times. (42 sts)

**Rnd 8:** *Sc 6, 2 sc in next sc*, rep 6 times. (48 sts)

**Rnd 9:** *Sc 7, 2 sc in next sc*, rep 6 times. (54 sts)

**Rnd 10:** *Sc 8, 2 sc in next sc*, rep 6 times. (60 sts)

**Rnd 11:** *Sc 9, 2 sc in next sc*, rep 6 times. (66 sts)

**Rnd 12:** *Sc 10, 2 sc in next sc*, rep 6 times. (72 sts)

**Rnd 13:** *Sc 11, 2 sc in next sc*, rep 6 times. (78 sts)

**Rnd 14:** *Sc 12, 2 sc in next sc*, rep 6 times. (84 sts)

**Rnds 15–31:** Sc 84.

**Rnd 32:** *Sc 12, dec 1*, rep 6 times. (78 sts)

**Rnd 33:** *Sc 11, dec 1*, rep 6 times. (72 sts)

**Rnd 34:** *Sc 10, dec 1*, rep 6 times. (66 sts)

**Rnd 35:** *Sc 9, dec 1*, rep 6 times. (60 sts)

**Rnd 36:** *Sc 8, dec 1*, rep 6 times. (54 sts)

**Work on face:** Stuff muzzle lightly. Use yarn and tapestry needle to sew muzzle in place at front of head. For dog, sew eye roundie to head. Position and attach plastic eyes with safety backings.

**Rnd 37:** *Sc 7, dec 1*, rep 6 times. (48 sts)

**Rnd 38:** *Sc 6, dec 1*, rep 6 times. (42 sts)

**Rnd 39:** *Sc 5, dec 1*, rep 6 times. (36 sts)

**Rnd 40:** *Sc 4, dec 1*, rep 6 times. (30 sts)

Stuff head.

**Rnd 41:** *Sc 3, dec 1*, rep 6 times. (24 sts)

**Rnd 42:** *Sc 2, dec 1*, rep 6 times. (18 sts)

**Rnd 43:** *Sc 1, dec 1*, rep 6 times. (12 sts)

**Rnd 44:** Dec 6 times. (6 sts)

Fasten off, leaving long tail to close up 6-st hole.

## DOG EAR

Make 2.

**Rnd 1:** Using tan yarn, ch 2, 5 sc in second ch from hook.

**Rnd 2:** Sc 2 in every sc around. (10 sts)

Rnd 3: *Sc 1, 2 sc in next sc*, rep 5 times. (15 sts)

Rnd 4: *Sc 2, 2 sc in next sc*, rep 5 times. (20 sts)

Rnds 5–15: Sc 20.

Rnd 16: *Sc 2, dec 1*, rep 5 times. (15 sts)

Rnds 17 and 18: Sc 15.

Sl st 1 and fasten off, leaving long tail for sewing. Sew open end closed and sew ears to head on rnd 15 on each side.

## CAT EAR

Make 2.

Rnd 1: Using white yarn, ch 2, 5 sc in second ch from hook.

Rnd 2: Sc 5.

Rnd 3: Sc 2 in every sc around. (10 sts)

Rnd 4: Sc 10.

Rnd 5: *Sc 1, 2 sc in next sc*, rep 5 times. (15 sts)

Rnd 6: Sc 15.

Rnd 7: *Sc 2, 2 sc in next sc*, rep 5 times. (20 sts)

Rnd 8: Sc 20.

Sl st 1 and fasten off, leaving long tail for sewing. Sew open end closed and sew ears to head starting on rnd 9 on each side.

## DOG BOW

Using medium-blue yarn, loosely ch 7.

Row 1: Sc 6 starting in second ch from hook, turn.

Rows 2–33: Ch 1, 6 sc, turn.

Fasten off. Fold rectangle in half and sew short ends tog. Wrap yarn around folded rectangle (horizontally) to form bow and, when you're happy with it, use yarn and tapestry needle to sew to dog's chin where head meets blanket.

## CAT BOW

Using light-pink yarn, loosely ch 5.

Row 1: Sc 4 starting in second ch from hook, turn.

Rows 2–19: Ch 1, 4 sc, turn.

Fasten off. Finish as for dog bow and sew to cat's ear.

## BLANKET BODY

Using tan yarn for dog or white yarn for cat, loosely ch 41.

Row 1: Sc 40 starting in second ch from hook, turn.

Rows 2–15: Ch 1, 40 sc, turn. Change to light-blue yarn for dog or light-pink yarn for cat.

Rows 16–18: Ch 2, 40 hdc, turn. Change to medium-blue yarn for dog or medium-pink yarn for cat.

Rows 19–21: Ch 2, 40 hdc, turn. Change to orange yarn for dog or green yarn for cat.

Rows 22–24: Ch 2, 40 hdc, turn. Change to light-blue yarn for dog or light-pink yarn for cat.

**Rows 25–51:** Rep rows 16–24 another 3 times. At end of row 51, change to tan yarn for dog or white yarn for cat.

**Rows 52–67:** Sc 1, 40 sc, turn. Fasten off for cat.

Cont for dog.

**Rows 68–70:** Sc 1, 40 sc, turn.

Fasten off.

## DOG FOOT

Make 4.

**Rnd 1:** Using tan yarn, ch 2, 6 sc in second ch from hook.

**Rnd 2:** Sc 2 in every sc around. (12 sts)

**Rnd 3:** *Sc 1, 2 sc in next sc*, rep 6 times. (18 sts)

**Rnds 4–12:** Sc 18.

Sl st 1 and fasten off, leaving long tail for sewing. Stuff a little, sew open end closed, and sew a foot to each corner of blanket.

## CAT FOOT

Make 4.

**Rnd 1:** Using white yarn, ch 2, 5 sc in second ch from hook.

**Rnd 2:** Sc 2 in every sc around. (10 sts)

**Rnd 3:** *Sc 1, 2 sc in next sc*, rep 5 times. (15 sts)

**Rnds 4–14:** Sc 15.

Sl st 1 and fasten off, leaving long tail for sewing. Stuff a little, sew open end closed, and sew a foot to each to corner of blanket.

## DOG TAIL

**Rnd 1:** Using tan yarn, ch 2, 5 sc in second ch from hook.

**Rnd 2:** Sc 2 in every sc around. (10 sts)

**Rnds 3–7:** Sc 10.

Sl st 1 and fasten off, leaving long tail for sewing. Sew open end closed and sew to blanket.

## CAT TAIL

**Rnd 1:** Using white yarn, ch 2, 6 sc in second ch from hook.

**Rnds 2–27:** Sc 6.

Sl st 1 and fasten off, leaving long tail for sewing. Sew open end closed and sew to blanket.

## FINISHING

**Dog:** Sew bottom of dog head, starting on rnd 33, to first 20 rows of blanket, centering head on blanket.

**Cat:** Sew bottom of cat head, starting on rnd 38, to first 4 rows of blanket, centering head on blanket.

# Tooth Fairy Pillow

*In Uruguay, where I'm from, it's not the Tooth Fairy that takes your tooth when it falls out but* Ratón Pérez *(a mouse called Pérez). The process is the same, though; kids leave their tooth under their pillow and* Ratón Pérez *leaves money for them. Sometimes, because he's really little, it's difficult for him to take the tooth from under the pillow because kids' heads are too heavy for him to lift. To be on the safe side, it's better to leave your tooth in a place that will make it easier for him to get it, like this little pillow. I bet the Tooth Fairy will appreciate it too!*

**FINISHED SIZE: APPROX 8" WIDE x 7½" TALL**

## MATERIALS

Worsted-weight yarn in white (approx 92 yds) and a small amount of pink

Size G-6 (4 mm) crochet hook

Black craft felt for eyes

Sewing thread and sharp needle

Tapestry needle

Black embroidery floss and embroidery needle

Fiberfill or stuffing of your choice

## POCKET INSERT

Using pink yarn, loosely ch 11.

**Row 1:** Sc 10 starting in second ch from hook, turn.

**Rows 2–10:** Ch 1, 10 sc, turn.

Fasten off, leaving long tail for sewing. Set aside.

## CHEEK

Make 2.

**Rnd 1:** Using pink yarn, ch 2, 6 sc in second ch from hook.

**Rnd 2:** Sc 2 in every sc around. (12 sts)

Sl st 1 and fasten off, leaving long tail for sewing. Set aside.

## TOOTH

Using white yarn, loosely ch 31.

**Rnd 1:** Sc 30 starting in second bump at back of ch (see page 72), then work 30 sc on opposite side of ch (front loops of ch). (60 sts)

**Rnds 2–10:** *Hdc 10, 20 sc*, rep twice.

**Rnds 11 and 12:** Sc 60.

**Rnd 13:** To make pocket opening, 15 sc, ch 8, sk 8 sts, 37 sc.

**Rnd 14:** Sc 15, 8 sc in ch-8 sp, 37 sc. (60 sts)

**Rnds 15–25:** Sc 60.

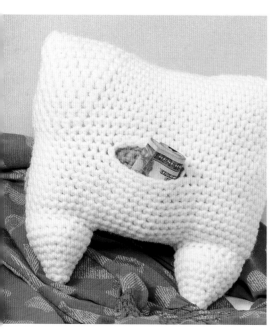

*A little pocket for the Tooth Fairy's gift of money.*

**Tooth fairy eye**

**Rnd 26:** Sc 5 to get to the corner, so it's neater to sew the bottom!

Fasten off, leaving long tail for sewing.

Turn pillow inside out, and align pocket with opening you left on rnd 13. Use yarn and tapestry needle to sew all around perimeter.

**Work on face:** Cut eyes from black felt. Use sewing thread and sharp needle to sew in place. Embroider smile. Use yarn and tapestry needle to sew cheeks to face.

Stuff tooth and sew open end closed.

## ROOT

Make 2.

**Rnd 1:** Using white yarn, ch 2, 5 sc in second ch from hook.

**Rnd 2:** Sc 5.

**Rnd 3:** Sc 2 in every sc around. (10 sts)

**Rnd 4:** Sc 10.

**Rnd 5:** *Sc 1, 2 sc in next sc*, rep 5 times. (15 sts)

**Rnd 6:** Sc 15.

**Rnd 7:** *Sc 2, 2 sc in next sc*, rep 5 times. (20 sts)

**Rnds 8 and 9:** Sc 20.

Sl st 1 and fasten off, leaving long tail for sewing. Stuff and sew root to each side of bottom of tooth.

## BOW

Using pink yarn, loosely ch 6.

**Row 1:** Sc 5 starting in second ch from hook, turn.

**Rows 2–11:** Ch 1, 5 sc, turn.

Fasten off. Weave in end.

Wrap yarn around middle of rectangle (horizontally) to form your bow and sew to top corner of tooth.

# Caterpillar Baskets

Keep your kids' desks organized and super cute with these little baskets that will hold everything from erasers to crayons to little dolls that help with homework.

⬆ FINISHED SIZE: **CATERPILLAR: APPROX 6" TALL x 16" LONG FROM HEAD TO TAIL BASKET: APPROX 2½" TALL x 3" IN DIAMETER**

## MATERIALS

Worsted-weight yarn in green (approx 186 yds), orange (approx 63 yds), and a small amount of pink* 🧶**4**

Size G-6 (4 mm) crochet hook

12 mm plastic eyes with safety backings

Black embroidery floss and embroidery needle

Tapestry needle

Fiberfill or stuffing of your choice

*Materials are enough for the caterpillar and three baskets. For each additional basket, you'll need approx 33 yds of green and 21 yds of orange yarn.*

## CATERPILLAR

Caterpillar is made in sections.

### Cheek

Make 2.

**Rnd 1:** Using pink yarn, ch 2, 6 sc in second ch from hook.

**Rnd 2:** Sc 2 in every sc around. (12 sts)

Sl st 1 and fasten off, leaving long tail for sewing. Set aside.

### Head

**Rnd 1:** Using green yarn, ch 2, 5 sc in second ch from hook.

**Rnd 2:** Sc 2 in every sc around. (10 sts)

**Rnd 3:** *Sc 1, 2 sc in next sc*, rep 5 times. (15 sts)

**Rnd 4:** *Sc 2, 2 sc in next sc*, rep 5 times. (20 sts)

**Rnd 5:** *Sc 3, 2 sc in next sc*, rep 5 times. (25 sts)

**Rnd 6:** *Sc 4, 2 sc in next sc*, rep 5 times. (30 sts)

**Rnd 7:** *Sc 5, 2 sc in next sc*, rep 5 times. (35 sts)

**Rnd 8:** *Sc 6, 2 sc in next sc*, rep 5 times. (40 sts)

**Rnd 9:** *Sc 7, 2 sc in next sc*, rep 5 times. (45 sts)

**Rnd 10:** *Sc 8, 2 sc in next sc*, rep 5 times. (50 sts)

**Rnd 11:** *Sc 9, 2 sc in next sc*, rep 5 times. (55 sts)

**Rnd 12:** *Sc 10, 2 sc in next sc*, rep 5 times. (60 sts)

**Rnd 13:** *Sc 11, 2 sc in next sc*, rep 5 times. (65 sts)

**Rnd 14:** *Sc 12, 2 sc in next sc*, rep 5 times. (70 sts)

**Rnd 15–31:** Sc 70.

**Rnd 32:** *Sc 12, dec 1*, rep 5 times. (65 sts)

**Rnd 33:** *Sc 11, dec 1*, rep 5 times. (60 sts)

**Rnd 34:** *Sc 10, dec 1*, rep 5 times. (55 sts)

**Rnd 35:** *Sc 9, dec 1*, rep 5 times. (50 sts)

**Rnd 36:** *Sc 8, dec 1*, rep 5 times. (45 sts)

**Work on face:** Position and attach plastic eyes with safety backings. Embroider smile. Use yarn and tapestry needle to sew cheeks to head.

**Rnd 37:** *Sc 7, dec 1*, rep 5 times. (40 sts)

**Rnd 38:** *Sc 6, dec 1*, rep 5 times. (35 sts)

**Rnd 39:** *Sc 5, dec 1*, rep 5 times. (30 sts)

**Rnd 40:** *Sc 4, dec 1*, rep 5 times. (25 sts)

Stuff head as much as you can.

**Rnd 41:** *Sc 3, dec 1*, rep 5 times. (20 sts)

**Rnd 42:** *Sc 2, dec 1*, rep 5 times. (15 sts)

Finish stuffing.

**Rnd 43:** *Sc 1, dec 1*, rep 5 times. (10 sts)

**Rnd 44:** Dec 5 times. (5 sts)

Fasten off, leaving long tail to close 5-st hole.

## Antenna

Make 2.

Join green yarn to spot where you want antenna to be. Ch 7 and fasten off.

# BASKET

Baskets are made in two parts. Make as many as you want.

## Outer Basket

**Rnd 1:** Using orange yarn, ch 2, 5 sc in second ch from hook.

**Rnd 2:** Sc 2 in every sc around. (10 sts)

**Rnd 3:** *Sc 1, 2 sc in next sc*, rep 5 times. (15 sts)

**Rnd 4:** *Sc 2, 2 sc in next sc*, rep 5 times. (20 sts)

**Rnd 5:** *Sc 3, 2 sc in next sc*, rep 5 times. (25 sts)

**Rnd 6:** *Sc 4, 2 sc in next sc*, rep 5 times. (30 sts)

**Rnd 7:** *Sc 5, 2 sc in next sc*, rep 5 times. (35 sts)

**Rnd 8:** *Sc 6, 2 sc in next sc*, rep 5 times. (40 sts)

**Rnds 9–11:** Sc 40.

Sl st 1 and fasten off, leaving long tail for sewing.

## Inner Basket

**Rnd 1:** Using green yarn, ch 2, 5 sc in second ch from hook.

**Rnd 2:** Sc 2 in every sc around. (10 sts)

**Rnd 3:** *Sc 1, 2 sc in next sc*, rep 5 times. (15 sts)

**Rnd 4:** *Sc 2, 2 sc in next sc*, rep 5 times. (20 sts)

**Rnd 5:** *Sc 3, 2 sc in next sc*, rep 5 times. (25 sts)

**Rnd 6:** *Sc 4, 2 sc in next sc*, rep 5 times. (30 sts)

**Rnd 7:** *Sc 5, 2 sc in next sc*, rep 5 times. (35 sts)

**Rnd 8:** *Sc 6, 2 sc in next sc*, rep 5 times. (40 sts)

**Rnds 9–15:** Sc 40.

Sl st 1 and fasten off.

Using long tail from outer basket, sew top edge of outer basket to bottom of inner basket.

# FINISHING

Use yarn and tapestry needle to sew baskets together side by side, then join one end of basket ch to side of caterpillar head on rnd 29.

# Cute Little Baskets

*Add a touch of whimsy to any place in your house with these cuties. Let them help you keep remote controls, little toys, fruit, or even toilet paper close at hand.*

**FINISHED SIZE: APPROX 5" TALL x 6" IN DIAMETER**

## MATERIALS

**Bunny basket:** Worsted-weight yarn in pink (approx 92 yds) and white (approx 22 yds)

Pink embroidery floss and embroidery needle

**Monster basket:** Worsted-weight yarn in blue (approx 88 yds) and green (approx 22 yds)

### For Both

Size J-10 (6 mm) crochet hook

Black and white craft felt for eyes and mouths

Sewing thread and sharp needle

Tapestry needle

## BASKET

**Rnd 1:** Using pink yarn for bunny or blue yarn for monster, ch 2, 5 sc in second ch from hook.

**Rnd 2:** Sc 2 in every sc around. (10 sts)

**Rnd 3:** *Sc 1, 2 sc in next sc*, rep 5 times. (15 sts)

**Rnd 4:** *Sc 2, 2 sc in next sc*, rep 5 times. (20 sts)

**Rnd 5:** *Sc 3, 2 sc in next sc*, rep 5 times. (25 sts)

**Rnd 6:** *Sc 4, 2 sc in next sc*, rep 5 times. (30 sts)

**Rnd 7:** *Sc 5, 2 sc in next sc*, rep 5 times. (35 sts)

**Rnd 8:** *Sc 6, 2 sc in next sc*, rep 5 times. (40 sts)

**Rnd 9:** *Sc 7, 2 sc in next sc*, rep 5 times. (45 sts)

**Rnd 10:** *Sc 8, 2 sc in next sc*, rep 5 times. (50 sts)

**Rnd 11:** *Sc 9, 2 sc in next sc*, rep 5 times. (55 sts)

**Rnd 12:** *Sc 10, 2 sc in next sc*, rep 5 times. (60 sts)

**Rnd 13:** *Sc 11, 2 sc in next sc*, rep 5 times. (65 sts)

**Rnd 14:** *Sc 12, 2 sc in next sc*, rep 5 times. (70 sts)

**Rnd 15:** *Sc 13, 2 sc in next sc*, rep 5 times. (75 sts)

**Rnds 16 and 17:** Sc 75.

**Rnd 18:** Sc 75 through back loops only (see page 72).

**Rnds 19–43:** Sc 75.

Sl st 1 and fasten off.

**Work on face:** Use patts on page 35. For bunny, cut eyes from black felt and muzzle from white felt. Using embroidery floss, embroider nose and smile on muzzle. Use sewing thread and sharp needle to sew eyes and muzzle on face. For monster, cut eyes and mouth from black felt and teeth from white felt. Sew teeth to mouth, then sew mouth and eyes to face.

## BUNNY EAR

Make 2.

**Rnd 1:** Using pink yarn, ch 2, 5 sc in second ch from hook.

**Rnd 2:** Sc 2 in every sc around. (10 sts)

**Rnd 3:** *Sc 1, 2 sc in next sc*, rep 5 times. (15 sts)

**Rnds 4–8:** Sc 15.

**Rnd 9:** *Sc 1, dec 1*, rep 5 times. (10 sts)

**Rnds 10–14:** Sc 10.

Sl st 1 and fasten off, leaving long tail for sewing. Using tapestry needle, sew open end closed and sew ears to bunny basket above face.

## MONSTER SPIKE

Make 4.

**Rnd 1:** Using green yarn, ch 2, 6 sc in second ch from hook.

**Rnd 2:** Sc 6.

**Rnd 3:** Sc 2 in every sc around. (12 sts)

**Rnds 4–6:** Sc 12.

Sl st 1 and fasten off, leaving long tail for sewing. Sew open end closed and sew spikes next to each other along top edge of monster basket above face.

## POCKET

For bunny, alternate 1 row white yarn and 1 row pink yarn, ending with white row. For monster, alternate 1 row green yarn and 1 row blue yarn, ending with green row.

Using white yarn for bunny or green yarn for monster, loosely ch 27.

**Row 1:** Sc 26 starting in second ch from hook, turn.

**Rows 2–17:** Ch 1, 26 sc, turn.

Fasten off.

Turn basket inside out. Using yarn and tapestry needle, sew pocket to back of basket, starting approx ½" from top edge, along sides and bottom. If desired, using yarn to match RS of basket, sew a line from top to bottom to divide pocket in half. Turn basket RS out and fill your baskets with fun stuff!

*Pockets create dividers for smaller items.*

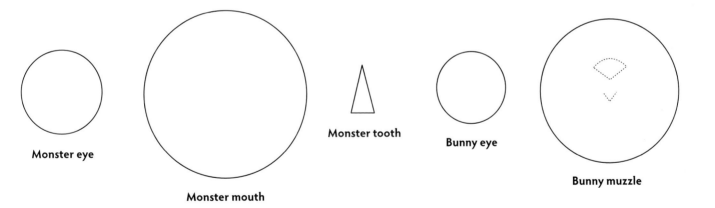

**Monster eye**

**Monster mouth**

**Monster tooth**

**Bunny eye**

**Bunny muzzle**

# Dinosaur Rug

*This little rug would look adorable in a nursery or in any room of the house as the designated baby, toddler, or even puppy spot! Federico (our smallest dog) wants it really bad, but one of my close friends is having a baby boy, so I made it for him. Sorry, Fico!*

**FINISHED SIZE: APPROX 16" x 20"**

## MATERIALS

Worsted-weight yarn in blue (approx 274 yds), green (approx 110 yds), yellow (approx 92 yds), purple (approx 22 yds), and a small amount of white

Size J-10 (6 mm) crochet hook

Black and white craft felt for eyes and mouth

Sewing thread and sharp needle

Tapestry needle

## RUG

Using blue yarn, loosely ch 71.

**Row 1:** Sc 70 starting in second ch from hook, turn.

**Rows 2–65:** Ch 1, 70 sc, turn. Fasten off.

### Top and Bottom Borders

Join yellow yarn to upper-right corner.

**Rows 1–4:** Ch 1, 70 sc, turn.

Fasten off. Weave in ends.

Rep rows 1–4 on opposite side of rug.

### Side Borders

Join yellow yarn to bottom-right corner at side.

**Rows 1–4:** Ch 1, 58 sc, turn.

Fasten off. Weave in ends.

Rep rows 1–4 on opposite side of rug.

## DINOSAUR

Dinosaur pieces are made separately and sewn to the rug.

### Head

**Rnd 1:** Using green yarn, ch 2, 6 sc in second ch from hook.

**Rnd 2:** Sc 2 in every sc around. (12 sts)

**Rnd 3:** *Sc 1, 2 sc in next sc*, rep 6 times. (18 sts)

**Rnd 4:** *Sc 2, 2 sc in next sc*, rep 6 times. (24 sts)

**Rnd 5:** *Sc 3, 2 sc in next sc*, rep 6 times. (30 sts)

**Rnd 6:** *Sc 4, 2 sc in next sc*, rep 6 times. (36 sts)

**Rnd 7:** *Sc 5, 2 sc in next sc*, rep 6 times. (42 sts)

**Rnd 8:** *Sc 6, 2 sc in next sc*, rep 6 times. (48 sts)

**Rnd 9:** *Sc 7, 2 sc in next sc*, rep 6 times. (54 sts)

**Rnd 10:** *Sc 8, 2 sc in next sc*, rep 6 times. (60 sts)

**Rnd 11:** *Sc 9, 2 sc in next sc*, rep 6 times. (66 sts)

**Rnd 12:** *Sc 10, 2 sc in next sc*, rep 6 times. (72 sts)

**Rnds 13–15:** Sc 72.

Sl st 1 and fasten off, leaving long tail for sewing.

## Body

Using green yarn, loosely ch 23.

**Row 1:** Sc 22 starting in second ch from hook, turn.

**Rows 2 and 3:** Ch 1, 22 sc, turn.

**Row 4:** Dec 1, 18 sc, dec 1, turn. (20 sts)

**Rows 5 and 6:** Ch 1, 20 sc, turn.

**Row 7:** Dec 1, 16 sc, dec 1, turn. (18 sts)

**Row 8:** Dec 1, 14 sc, dec 1, turn. (16 sts)

**Rows 9–11:** Ch 1, 16 sc, turn.

**Row 12:** Dec 1, 12 sc, dec 1, turn. (14 sts)

**Row 13:** Ch 1, 14 sc, turn.

**Row 14:** Dec 1, 10 sc, dec 1, turn. (12 sts)

**Row 15:** Dec 1, 8 sc, dec 1, turn. (10 sts)

**Row 16:** Ch 1, 10 sc, turn.

**Row 17:** Dec 1, 6 sc, dec 1, turn. (8 sts)

Fasten off. Weave in ends.

Join green yarn to first stitch of row 1 on bottom-right edge of body, 15 sc to top, 8 sc across top, 15 sc down left edge of body. Fasten off.

## Neck

Using green yarn, loosely ch 4.

**Row 1:** Sc 3 starting in second ch from hook, turn.

**Rows 2–24:** Ch 1, 3 sc, turn.

Fasten off, leaving long tail for sewing.

## Leg

Make 4.

Using green yarn, loosely ch 6.

**Row 1:** Sc 5 starting in second ch from hook, turn.

**Rows 2 and 3:** Ch 1, 5 sc, turn.

**Row 4:** Dec 1, 1 sc, dec 1, turn. (3 sts)

**Rows 5–7:** Ch 1, 3 sc, turn.

Fasten off, leaving long tail for sewing.

## Spike

Make 8.

Using purple yarn, loosely ch 5.

**Row 1:** Sc 4 starting in second ch from hook, turn.

**Rows 2 and 3:** Ch 1, 4 sc, turn.

**Row 4:** Dec twice. (2 sts)

**Row 5:** Dec once. (1 st)

Fasten off, leaving long tail for sewing.

## FINISHING

Referring to photo on page 36, position pieces as shown, placing neck under head and body pieces. Using yarn and tapestry needle, sew neck, head, body, and feet in place. Sew 6 spikes along top edge of body. Sew 1 spike on each side of head for ears.

Cut eye circles from black and white felt, and mouth from black felt (patts at right). Using sewing thread and sharp needle, sew small white circle to black circle, and then sew both to large white circle. Sew mouth and eyes to face. Using white yarn and tapestry needle, embroider 2 long sts next to each other to make each of 3 toes on legs.

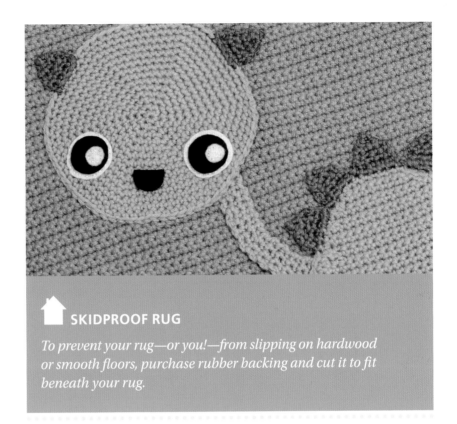

### 🏠 SKIDPROOF RUG

*To prevent your rug—or you!—from slipping on hardwood or smooth floors, purchase rubber backing and cut it to fit beneath your rug.*

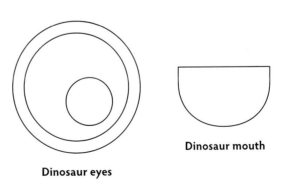

**Dinosaur eyes**

**Dinosaur mouth**

# Cupcake Rug

*Even though I crocheted it with kids in mind, I'm thinking this little cupcake would look great in the kitchen (my kitchen!) in front of the sink—Oli washes the dishes sometimes, so I can always pretend I did it for her, no?*

**FINISHED SIZE: APPROX 17" WIDE x 18" TALL**

## MATERIALS

Worsted-weight yarn in pink (approx 220 yds), tan (approx 110 yds), red (approx 22 yds), and a small amount of brown

Size J-10 (6 mm) crochet hook

Black craft felt for eyes and smiles

Sewing thread and sharp needle

Tapestry needle

## CUPCAKE

Using tan yarn, loosely ch 56.

**Row 1:** Sc 55 starting in second ch from hook, turn.

**Row 2:** Ch 1, 55 sc, turn.

**Row 3:** Ch 1, 2 sc in first sc, 53 sc, 2 sc in last sc. (57 sts)

**Rows 4–25:** Ch 1, 57 sc, turn.

Change to pink yarn.

**Row 26:** Ch 1, 2 sc in first sc, 55 sc, 2 sc in last sc, turn. (59 sts)

**Row 27:** Through back loops only (see page 72), ch 1, 2 sc in first sc, 57 sc, 2 sc in last sc, turn. (61 sts)

**Row 28:** Ch 1, 2 sc in first sc, 59 sc, 2 sc in last sc, turn. (63 sts)

**Rows 29–60:** Ch 1, 63 sc, turn.

**Row 61:** Dec 1, 59 sc, dec 1, turn. (61 sts)

**Row 62:** Ch 1, 61 sc, turn.

**Row 63:** Dec 1, 57 sc, dec 1, turn. (59 sts)

**Row 64:** Ch 1, 59 sc, turn.

**Row 65:** Dec 1, 55 sc, dec 1, turn. (57 sts)

**Row 66:** Ch 1, 57 sc, turn.

**Row 67:** Dec 1, 53 sc, dec 1, turn. (55 sts)

**Row 68:** Ch 1, 55 sc, turn.

**Row 69:** Dec 1, 51 sc, dec 1, turn. (53 sts)

**Row 70:** Ch 1, 53 sc, turn.

**Row 71:** Dec 1, 49 sc, dec 1, turn. (51 sts)

**Row 72:** Ch 1, 51 sc, turn.

**Row 73:** Dec 1, 47 sc, dec 1, turn. (49 sts)

**Row 74:** Ch 1, 49 sc, turn.

**Row 75:** Dec 1, 45 sc, dec 1, turn. (47 sts)

*Pink edging separates the frosting from the cake.*

Row 76: Dec 1, 43 sc, dec 1, turn. (45 sts)

Row 77: Dec 1, 41 sc, dec 1, turn. (43 sts)

Row 78: Dec 1, 39 sc, dec 1, turn. (41 sts)

Row 79: Dec 1, 37 sc, dec 1, turn. (39 sts)

Row 80: Dec 1, 35 sc, dec 1, turn. (37 sts)

Row 81: Dec 1, 33 sc, dec 1, turn. (35 sts)

Row 82: Dec 1, 31 sc, dec 1, turn. (33 sts)

Row 83: Dec 1, 29 sc, dec 1, turn. (31 sts)

Fasten off.

## EDGING

Join pink yarn on right edge of rug at row 26 (where tan and pink yarns meet). Sc 60 to top (until you reach row 83), 31 sc across top of cupcake, then 60 sc down left side. Fasten off.

Join pink yarn to front loops of row 27 and work as follows.

Row 1: Sl st 1, *hdc 1, 1 dc, 3 tr, sl st 1*, rep 10 times. Fasten off.

Row 2: Join yarn to first st of row 1, *2 sc, 2 sc in next tr, 2 sc, 1 sc in same st you worked sl st in row 1*, rep 9 times, 2 sc, 2 sc in next tr, 2 sc, sl st 1 in first sc of sc edge around top. Fasten off.

## CHERRY

Rnd 1: Using red yarn, ch 2, 5 sc in second ch from hook.

Rnd 2: Sc 2 in every sc around. (10 sts)

Rnd 3: *Sc 1, 2 sc in next sc*, rep 5 times. (15 sts)

Rnd 4: *Sc 2, 2 sc in next sc*, rep 5 times. (20 sts)

Rnd 5: *Sc 3, 2 sc in next sc*, rep 5 times. (25 sts)

Rnd 6: *Sc 4, 2 sc in next sc*, rep 5 times. (30 sts)

Rnd 7: *Sc 5, 2 sc in next sc*, rep 5 times. (35 sts)

Rnd 8: *Sc 6, 2 sc in next sc*, rep 5 times. (40 sts)

Rnd 9: *Sc 7, 2 sc in next sc*, rep 5 times. (45 sts)

**Rnd 10:** Sc 45.

Sl st 1 and fasten off.

For stem, join brown yarn at edge of cherry, loosely ch 6. Sl st 5 starting in second ch from hook and working under 2 loops on back of ch. Fasten off.

## FINISHING

Use patts below.

Cut cherry eyes and smile from black felt. Using sewing thread and sharp needle, sew eyes and smile to cherry. Using yarn and tapestry needle, sew cherry to upper-right corner of rug.

Cut cupcake eyes and smile from black felt and sew to tan portion of rug.

**SAFETY TIP**

*If you plan to use your rug on hardwood or smooth floors, prevent slippage by buying rubber backing and cutting it to fit beneath your rug.*

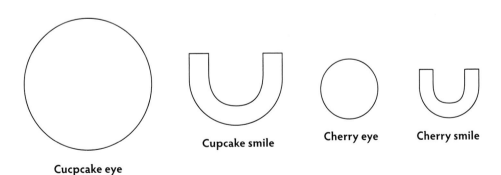

**Cucpcake eye**

**Cupcake smile**

**Cherry eye**

**Cherry smile**

# Little Teacup Rug

*This one's for your kitchen! My relationship with dishwashing is definitely complicated. I either don't mind it or I hate it with all my being. I don't even know what my feelings depend on. It's not about the amount of dirty things piled in the sink, or the time of day, or my mood—sometimes I just do not want to wash dishes. Period. Still, I'm positive that a smiling cup will make it a lot easier on the "hate days."*

**FINISHED SIZE: APPROX 13" TALL x 19" WIDE**

## MATERIALS

Worsted-weight yarn in sky blue (approx 328 yds)

Size J-10 (6 mm) crochet hook

Black craft felt for eyes and smile

Sewing thread and sharp needle

Tapestry needle

## CUP

Using sky-blue yarn, loosely ch 71.

**Row 1:** Sc 70 starting in second ch from hook, turn.

**Rows 2–30:** Ch 1, 70 sc, turn.

**Row 31:** Dec 1, 66 sc, dec 1, turn. (68 sts)

**Row 32:** Ch 1, 68 sc, turn.

**Row 33:** Dec 1, 64 sc, dec 1, turn. (66 sts)

**Row 34:** Ch 1, 66 sc, turn.

**Row 35:** Dec 1, 62 sc, dec 1, turn. (64 sts)

**Row 36:** Ch 1, 64 sc, turn.

**Row 37:** Dec 1, 60 sc, dec 1, turn. (62 sts)

**Row 38:** Ch 1, 62 sc, turn.

**Row 39:** Dec 1, 58 sc, dec 1, turn. (60 sts)

**Row 40:** Ch 1, 60 sc, turn.

**Row 41:** Dec 1, 56 sc, dec 1, turn. (58 sts)

**Row 42:** Ch 1, 58 sc, turn.

**Row 43:** Dec 1, 54 sc, dec 1, turn. (56 sts)

**Row 44:** Ch 1, 56 sc, turn.

**Row 45:** Dec 1, 52 sc, dec 1, turn. (54 sts)

**Row 46:** Ch 1, 54 sc, turn.

**Row 47:** Dec 1, 50 sc, dec 1, turn. (52 sts)

**Row 48:** Ch 1, 52 sc, turn.

**Row 49:** Dec 1, 48 sc, dec 1, turn. (50 sts)

*Stitch the ends of the handle ½" from the edge.*

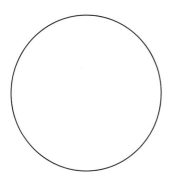

**Teacup eye**

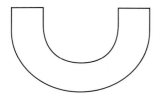

**Teacup smile**

🏠 **WATCH YOUR STEP!**

*Avoid slippage on hardwood or smooth floors by purchasing rubber backing and cutting it to fit under your rug.*

**Row 50:** Ch 1, 50 sc, turn.

**Row 51:** Dec 1, 46 sc, dec 1, turn. (48 sts)

**Row 52:** Ch 1, 48 sc, turn.

**Row 53:** Dec 1, 44 sc, dec 1, turn. (46 sts)

**Row 54:** Ch 1, 46 sc, turn.

**Row 55:** Dec 1, 42 sc, dec 1, turn. (44 sts)

**Row 56:** Ch 1, 44 sc, turn.

**Row 57:** Dec 1, 40 sc, dec 1, turn. (42 sts)

**Row 58:** Ch 1, 42 sc, turn.

**Row 59:** Dec 1, 38 sc, dec 1, turn. (40 sts)

Fasten off.

Position teacup with wide edge at top and join yarn to upper-right corner. Sc 70 across top, work 2 sc in last sc, 58 sc along left side, 40 sc across bottom, and 58 sc on along right side, work 2 sc in last st. Sl st 1 and fasten off.

## HANDLE

Using sky-blue yarn, loosely ch 27, leaving long tail for sewing.

Starting in third ch from hook, 8 hdc, 3 hdc in next st, 7 hdc, 3 hdc in next st, 8 hdc.

Fasten off, leaving long tail for sewing. Use tapestry needle to sew ends of handle to cup, starting about 2" from upper-right corner and ½" in from edge.

## FINISHING

Cut eyes and smile from black felt (patts at left). Using sewing thread and sharp needle, sew eyes and smile to narrow portion of rug referring to photo on page 44.

# Mushroom Floor Cushion

*Crochet this one, close your eyes, and imagine you're in Wonderland with Alice! (Or with Super Mario in whatever his land is called.) Your kids will love it regardless and it will make a special place for them to sit, read, and dream.*

 **FINISHED SIZE: APPROX 6½" TALL x 14" IN DIAMETER**

## MATERIALS

Worsted-weight yarn in white (approx 350 yds) and red (approx 328 yds) **4**

Size J-10 (6 mm) crochet hook

Tapestry needle

14"-long zipper

Sewing thread and sharp needle

Fiberfill or a round pillow approx 6" tall x 14" diameter

## TOP

**Rnd 1:** Using red yarn, ch 2, 6 sc in second ch from hook.

**Rnd 2:** Sc 2 in every sc around. (12 sts)

**Rnd 3:** *Sc 1, 2 sc in next sc*, rep 6 times. (18 sts)

**Rnd 4:** *Sc 2, 2 sc in next sc*, rep 6 times. (24 sts)

**Rnd 5:** *Sc 3, 2 sc in next sc*, rep 6 times. (30 sts)

**Rnd 6:** *Sc 4, 2 sc in next sc*, rep 6 times. (36 sts)

**Rnd 7:** *Sc 5, 2 sc in next sc*, rep 6 times. (42 sts)

**Rnd 8:** *Sc 6, 2 sc in next sc*, rep 6 times. (48 sts)

**Rnd 9:** *Sc 7, 2 sc in next sc*, rep 6 times. (54 sts)

**Rnd 10:** *Sc 8, 2 sc in next sc*, rep 6 times. (60 sts)

**Rnd 11:** *Sc 9, 2 sc in next sc*, rep 6 times. (66 sts)

**Rnd 12:** *Sc 10, 2 sc in next sc*, rep 6 times. (72 sts)

**Rnd 13:** *Sc 11, 2 sc in next sc*, rep 6 times. (78 sts)

**Rnd 14:** *Sc 12, 2 sc in next sc*, rep 6 times. (84 sts)

**Rnd 15:** *Sc 13, 2 sc in next sc*, rep 6 times. (90 sts)

**Rnd 16:** *Sc 14, 2 sc in next sc*, rep 6 times. (96 sts)

**Rnd 17:** *Sc 15, 2 sc in next sc*, rep 6 times. (102 sts)

**Rnd 18:** *Sc 16, 2 sc in next sc*, rep 6 times. (108 sts)

**Rnd 19:** *Sc 17, 2 sc in next sc*, rep 6 times. (114 sts)

**Rnd 20:** *Sc 18, 2 sc in next sc*, rep 6 times. (120 sts)

**Rnd 21:** *Sc 19, 2 sc in next sc*, rep 6 times. (126 sts)

**Rnd 22:** *Sc 20, 2 sc in next sc*, rep 6 times. (132 sts)

**Rnds 23–35:** Sc 132.

**Rnd 36:** Sc 132 through back loops only (see page 72).

Sl st 1 and fasten off.

## BOTTOM

Using white yarn, work rnds 1–31 as for top.

Sl st and fasten off.

## SPOTS

Make 3 small and 7 large spots, or whatever number you desire.

### Small

**Rnd 1:** Using white yarn, ch 2, 5 sc in second ch from hook.

**Rnd 2:** Sc 2 in every sc around. (10 sts)

**Rnd 3:** *Sc 1, 2 sc in next sc*, rep 5 times. (15 sts)

Sl st 1 and fasten off, leaving long tail for sewing. Set aside.

### Large

**Rnd 1:** Using white yarn, ch 2, 5 sc in second ch from hook.

**Rnd 2:** Sc 2 in every sc around. (10 sts)

**Rnd 3:** *Sc 1, 2 sc in next sc*, rep 5 times. (15 sts)

**Rnd 4:** *Sc 2, 2 sc in next sc*, rep 5 times. (20 sts)

**Rnd 5:** *Sc 3, 2 sc in next sc*, rep 5 times. (25 sts)

Sl st 1 and fasten off, leaving long tail for sewing. Set aside.

## FINISHING

**Sew spots:** Using yarn and tapestry needle, sew spots randomly on top of mushroom.

**Zipper:** With zipper closed, baste it in place between top and bottom with sewing needle and contrasting-color sewing thread. Sew zipper in place with tapestry needle and yarn to match top and bottom. Sew one side, then open zipper and sew other side. Sew remainder of seam between top and bottom all around.

**Ruffle:** Join red yarn to 1 of front loops you left unworked in rnd 36 of top, and work ruffle as follows.

**Rnd 1:** Sc 132 through front loops only.

**Rnds 2–8:** Sc 132.

Fold ruffle in half and sew rnd 8 to rnd 1 all around.

Stuff to make a comfortable cushion.

# Ladybug Floor Cushion

*This one will look great in a kids' room, a nursery, and even in the backyard. Crochet a couple and let the kids pretend to be flying with the birds, the butterflies, and other ladybug friends!*

**FINISHED SIZE: APPROX 8" TALL x 15" IN DIAMETER**

## MATERIALS

Worsted-weight yarn in red (approx 350 yds), black (approx 220 yds), and white (approx 22 yds)

Size J-10 (6 mm) crochet hook

14"-long zipper

Sewing thread and sharp needle

12 mm plastic eyes with safety backings

Tapestry needle

Red embroidery floss and embroidery needle

Fiberfill or round pillow form approx 8" tall x 15" diameter

## TOP

**Rnd 1:** Using red yarn, ch 2, 5 sc in second ch from hook.

**Rnd 2:** Sc 2 in every sc around. (10 sts)

**Rnd 3:** *Sc 1, 2 sc in next sc*, rep 5 times. (15 sts)

**Rnd 4:** *Sc 2, 2 sc in next sc*, rep 5 times. (20 sts)

**Rnd 5:** Sc 20.

**Rnd 6:** *Sc 1, 2 sc in next sc*, rep 10 times. (30 sts)

**Rnd 7:** Sc 30.

**Rnd 8:** *Sc 2, 2 sc in next sc*, rep 10 times. (40 sts)

**Rnd 9:** Sc 40.

**Rnd 10:** *Sc 3, 2 sc in next sc*, rep 10 times. (50 sts)

**Rnd 11:** Sc 50.

**Rnd 12:** *Sc 4, 2 sc in next sc*, rep 10 times. (60 sts)

**Rnd 13:** Sc 60.

**Rnd 14:** *Sc 5, 2 sc in next sc*, rep 10 times. (70 sts)

**Rnd 15:** Sc 70.

**Rnd 16:** *Sc 6, 2 sc in next sc*, rep 10 times. (80 sts)

**Rnd 17:** Sc 80.

**Rnd 18:** *Sc 7, 2 sc in next sc*, rep 10 times. (90 sts)

**Rnd 19:** Sc 90.

**Rnd 20:** *Sc 8, 2 sc in next sc*, rep 10 times. (100 sts)

**Rnd 21:** Sc 100.

**Rnd 22:** *Sc 9, 2 sc in next sc*, rep 10 times. (110 sts)

**Rnd 23:** Sc 110.

**Rnd 24:** *Sc 10, 2 sc in next sc*, rep 10 times. (120 sts)

**Rnd 25:** Sc 120.

**Rnd 26:** *Sc 11, 2 sc in next sc*, rep 10 times. (130 sts)

**Rnd 27:** Sc 130.

**Rnd 28:** *Sc 12, 2 sc in next sc*, rep 10 times. (140 sts)

**Rnds 29–45:** Sc 140.

**Rnd 46:** Sc 140 through back loops only (see page 72).

Sl st 1 and fasten off.

## BOTTOM

Using black yarn, work rnds 1–28 as for top.

**Rnds 29–31:** Sc 140.

Sl st 1 and fasten off.

**Zipper:** With zipper closed, baste it in place between top and bottom with sewing needle and contrasting-color sewing thread. Sew zipper in place with tapestry needle and yarn to match top or bottom. Sew one side, then open zipper and sew other side. Sew remainder of seam between top and bottom all around.

**Ruffle:** Join red yarn to 1 of the front loops you left unworked on rnd 46 of top, and work ruffle as follows:

**Rnd 1:** Sc 140 through front loops only.

**Rnd 2:** Sc 140.

Fasten off.

## EYE

Make 2.

**Rnd 1:** Using white yarn, ch 2, 5 sc in second ch from hook.

**Rnd 2:** Sc 2 in every sc around. (10 sts)

**Rnd 3:** *Sc 1, 2 sc in next sc*, rep 5 times. (15 sts)

**Rnds 4 and 5:** Sc 15.

Sl st 1 and fasten off, leaving long tail for sewing. Attach plastic eye with safety backing to center of eye. Set aside.

## HEAD

**Rnd 1:** Using black yarn, ch 2, 5 sc in second ch from hook.

**Rnd 2:** Sc 2 in every sc around. (10 sts)

**Rnd 3:** *Sc 1, 2 sc in next sc*, rep 5 times. (15 sts)

**Rnd 4:** *Sc 2, 2 sc in next sc*, rep 5 times. (20 sts)

**Rnd 5:** *Sc 3, 2 sc in next sc*, rep 5 times. (25 sts)

*amigurumi at home*

**Rnd 6:** *Sc 4, 2 sc in next sc*, rep 5 times. (30 sts)

**Rnd 7:** *Sc 5, 2 sc in next sc*, rep 5 times. (35 sts)

**Rnd 8:** *Sc 6, 2 sc in next sc*, rep 5 times. (40 sts)

**Rnd 9:** *Sc 7, 2 sc in next sc*, rep 5 times. (45 sts)

**Rnd 10:** *Sc 8, 2 sc in next sc*, rep 5 times. (50 sts)

**Rnd 11:** *Sc 9, 2 sc in next sc*, rep 5 times. (55 sts)

**Rnd 12:** *Sc 10, 2 sc in next sc*, rep 5 times. (60 sts)

**Rnds 13–19:** Sc 60.

**Rnd 20:** *Sc 10, dec 1*, rep 5 times. (55 sts)

**Rnd 21:** *Sc 9, dec 1*, rep 5 times. (50 sts)

Sl st 1 and fasten off, leaving long tail for sewing. Stuff eyes lightly and sew in place. Embroider mouth. Sew head to front of body between rnds 27 and 45 on opposite side of where zipper was sewn.

## SPOT

Make 10.

**Rnd 1:** Using black yarn, ch 2, 6 sc in second ch from hook.

**Rnd 2:** Sc 2 in every sc around. (12 sts)

**Rnd 3:** *Sc 1, 2 sc in next sc*, rep 6 times. (18 sts)

**Rnd 4:** *Sc 2, 2 sc in next sc*, rep 6 times. (24 sts)

**Rnd 5:** *Sc 3, 2 sc in next sc*, rep 6 times. (30 sts)

Sl st 1 and fasten off, leaving long tail for sewing. Set aside.

## ANTENNA

Make 2.

Join black yarn about 1½" above center of eye, ch 13, sl st 12 working through 2 loops on back of ch, fasten off.

## FOOT

Make 6.

**Rnd 1:** Using black yarn, ch 2, 7 sc in second ch from hook.

**Rnd 2:** Sc 2 in every sc around. (14 sts)

**Rnds 3–10:** Sc 14.

Sl st 1 and fasten off, leaving long tail for sewing. Sew open end closed and sew feet to body (3 on each side).

## FINISHING

**Body line:** Using black yarn and crochet hook, crochet a line of ch stitches (see below) in middle of red top from back of cushion to back of head. With yarn on inside of cushion, insert hook in a st on last rnd of ruffle, yarn over hook, and pull through to outside. *Insert hook in next st 1 rnd above, yarn over hook, pull through to outside, then pull through loop on hook. Repeat from * to back of head. Fasten off. Note that you can also embroider the line with tapestry needle and black yarn.

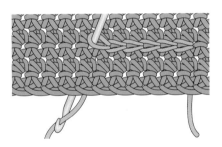

**Sew spots:** Sew 5 spots on each side of body line, referring to photo on page 50.

Stuff to make a comfortable cushion.

# Cloud Pillow

*Oli claimed this one, so as you read this, it'll be on her bed. I think I'm going to make myself one too. I love clouds and cloud-shaped stuff and it would look super adorable on our blue couch. I bet any new mom would love one for her baby's room too!*

 **FINISHED SIZE: APPROX 12" TALL x 21" WIDE**

## MATERIALS

Worsted-weight yarn in white (approx 656 yds) **4**

Size K-10½ (6.5 mm) crochet hook

Pink and black craft felt for eyes and cheeks

Sewing thread and sharp needle

Black embroidery floss and embroidery needle

Tapestry needle

Fiberfill or stuffing of your choice

## CLOUD

**Rnd 1:** Using white yarn, ch 2, 5 sc in second ch from hook.

**Rnd 2:** Sc 2 in every sc around. (10 sts)

**Rnd 3:** *Sc 1, 2 sc in next sc*, rep 5 times. (15 sts)

**Rnd 4:** *Sc 2, 2 sc in next sc*, rep 5 times. (20 sts)

**Rnd 5:** *Sc 3, 2 sc in next sc*, rep 5 times. (25 sts)

**Rnd 6:** *Sc 4, 2 sc in next sc*, rep 5 times. (30 sts)

**Rnd 7:** *Sc 5, 2 sc in next sc*, rep 5 times. (35 sts)

**Rnd 8:** *Sc 6, 2 sc in next sc*, rep 5 times. (40 sts)

**Rnd 9:** *Sc 7, 2 sc in next sc*, rep 5 times. (45 sts)

**Rnd 10:** *Sc 8, 2 sc in next sc*, rep 5 times. (50 sts)

**Rnd 11:** *Sc 9, 2 sc in next sc*, rep 5 times. (55 sts)

**Rnd 12:** *Sc 10, 2 sc in next sc*, rep 5 times. (60 sts)

**Rnd 13:** *Sc 11, 2 sc in next sc*, rep 5 times. (65 sts)

**Rnd 14:** *Sc 12, 2 sc in next sc*, rep 5 times. (70 sts)

**Rnd 15:** *Sc 13, 2 sc in next sc*, rep 5 times. (75 sts)

**Rnd 16:** *Sc 14, 2 sc in next sc*, rep 5 times. (80 sts)

**Rnd 17:** Sc 80.

**Rnd 18:** Sc 3 in next sc, 79 sc. (82 sts)

**Rnd 19:** Sc 3 in next sc, 1 sc, 3 sc in next sc, 79 sc. (86 sts)

**Rnd 20:** Sc 3, 3 sc in next sc, 82 sc. (88 sts)

**Rnd 21:** Sc 3, 3 sc in next sc, 1 sc, 3 sc in next sc, 82 sc. (92 sts)

**Rnd 22:** Sc 6, 3 sc in next sc, 85 sc. (94 sts)

**Rnds 23–29:** Sc 94.

**Rnd 30:** Sc 7, dec 1, 85 sc. (93 sts)

**Rnd 31:** Sc 5, dec 1, 2 sc, dec 1, 82 sc. (91 sts)

**Rnd 32:** Sc 6, dec 1, 83 sc. (90 sts)

**Rnd 33:** Sc 4, dec 1, 2 sc, dec 1, 80 sc. (88 sts)

**Rnd 34:** Sc 5, dec 1, 81 sc. (87 sts)

**Rnd 35:** Sc 3, dec 1, 2 sc, dec 1, 78 sc. (85 sts)

**Rnd 36:** Sc 3, dec 1, 80 sc. (84 sts)

**Rnd 37:** Sc 84.

**Rnd 38:** Sc 4, 3 sc in next sc, 79 sc. (86 sts)

**Rnd 39:** Sc 86.

**Rnd 40:** Sc 4, 3 sc in next sc, 1 sc, 3 sc in next sc, 79 sc. (90 sts)

**Rnd 41:** Sc 90.

**Rnd 42:** Sc 7, 3 sc in next sc, 82 sc. (92 sts)

**Rnd 43:** Sc 92.

**Rnd 44:** Sc 7, 3 sc in next sc, 1 sc, 3 sc in next sc, 82 sc. (96 sts)

**Rnd 45:** Sc 96.

**Rnd 46:** Sc 10, 3 sc in next sc, 85 sc. (98 sts)

**Rnds 47–64:** Sc 98.

**Rnd 65:** Sc 12, dec 1, 84 sc. (97 sts)

**Rnd 66:** Sc 10, dec 1, 2 sc, dec 1, 81 sc. (95 sts)

**Rnd 67:** Sc 95.

**Rnd 68:** Sc 11, dec 1, 82 sc. (94 sts)

**Rnd 69:** Sc 9, dec 1, 2 sc, dec 1, 79 sc. (92 sts)

**Rnd 70:** Sc 92.

**Rnd 71:** Sc 10, dec 1, 80 sc. (91 sts)

**Rnd 72:** Sc 8, dec 1, 2 sc, dec 1, 77 sc. (89 sts)

**Rnd 73:** Sc 9, dec 1, 78 sc. (88 sts)

**Rnd 74:** Sc 88.

**Rnd 75:** Sc 7, dec 1, 2 sc, dec 1, 75 sc. (86 sts)

**Rnd 76:** Sc 8, dec 1, 76 sc. (85 sts)

**Rnd 77:** Sc 6, dec 1, 2 sc, dec 1, 73 sc. (83 sts)

**Rnd 78:** Sc 83.

**Rnd 79:** Sc 7, dec 1, 74 sc. (82 sts)

**Rnd 80:** Sc 5, dec 1, 2 sc, dec 1, 71 sc. (80 sts)

**Rnd 81:** Sc 80.

**Rnd 82:** *Sc 14, dec 1*, rep 5 times. (75 sts)

**Rnd 83:** *Sc 13, dec 1*, rep 5 times. (70 sts)

**Rnd 84:** *Sc 12, dec 1*, rep 5 times. (65 sts)

**Work on face:** Cut cheeks from pink felt and eyes from black felt (patts on page 57). Use sewing thread and sharp needle to sew in place. Embroider mouth.

Stuff almost to top.

**Rnd 85:** *Sc 11, dec 1*, rep 5 times. (60 sts)

**Rnd 86:** *Sc 10, dec 1*, rep 5 times. (55 sts)

**Rnd 87:** *Sc 9, dec 1*, rep 5 times. (50 sts)

**Rnd 88:** *Sc 8, dec 1*, rep 5 times. (45 sts)

**Rnd 89:** *Sc 7, dec 1*, rep 5 times. (40 sts)

**Rnd 90:** *Sc 6, dec 1*, rep 5 times. (35 sts)

**Rnd 91:** *Sc 5, dec 1*, rep 5 times. (30 sts)

Stuff again.

**Rnd 92:** *Sc 4, dec 1*, rep 5 times. (25 sts)

**Rnd 93:** *Sc 3, dec 1*, rep 5 times. (20 sts)

**Rnd 94:** *Sc 2, dec 1*, rep 5 times. (15 sts)

**Rnd 95:** *Sc 1, dec 1*, rep 5 times. (10 sts)

Finish stuffing.

**Rnd 96:** Dec 5 times. (5 sts)

Fasten off, leaving long tail and use it to close 5-st hole.

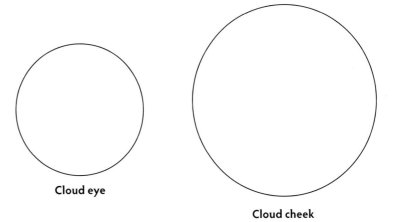

**Cloud eye**

**Cloud cheek**

# Turtle Floor Cushion

*Turtles are my favorite animal and I could not resist crocheting a big one to have around. Pick the colors of the shell to match your decor and you'll have an instant favorite sitting spot wherever your turtle decides to live.*

**FINISHED SIZE: APPROX 6½" TALL x 12" IN DIAMETER**

## MATERIALS

Worsted-weight yarn in orange (approx 328 yds), red (approx 110 yds), and a small amount of pink

Chunky-weight yarn in green (approx 88 yds) **5**

Size H-8 (5 mm) crochet hook

Size I-9 (5.5 mm) crochet hook

12 mm plastic eyes with safety backings

Black embroidery floss and embroidery needle

Tapestry needle

Fiberfill or stuffing of your choice

## SHELL TOP

Start with orange, and alternate 1 rnd orange and 1 rnd red throughout.

**Rnd 1:** Using H hook, ch 2, 6 sc in second ch from hook.

**Rnd 2:** Sc 2 in every sc around. (12 sts)

**Rnd 3:** *Sc 1, 2 sc in next sc*, rep 6 times. (18 sts)

**Rnd 4:** *Sc 2, 2 sc in next sc*, rep 6 times. (24 sts)

**Rnd 5:** *Sc 3, 2 sc in next sc*, rep 6 times. (30 sts)

**Rnd 6:** *Sc 4, 2 sc in next sc*, rep 6 times. (36 sts)

**Rnd 7:** *Sc 5, 2 sc in next sc*, rep 6 times. (42 sts)

**Rnd 8:** *Sc 6, 2 sc in next sc*, rep 6 times. (48 sts)

**Rnd 9:** *Sc 7, 2 sc in next sc*, rep 6 times. (54 sts)

**Rnd 10:** *Sc 8, 2 sc in next sc*, rep 6 times. (60 sts)

**Rnd 11:** *Sc 9, 2 sc in next sc*, rep 6 times. (66 sts)

**Rnd 12:** *Sc 10, 2 sc in next sc*, rep 6 times. (72 sts)

**Rnd 13:** *Sc 11, 2 sc in next sc*, rep 6 times. (78 sts)

**Rnd 14:** *Sc 12, 2 sc in next sc*, rep 6 times. (84 sts)

**Rnd 15:** *Sc 13, 2 sc in next sc*, rep 6 times. (90 sts)

**Rnd 16:** *Sc 14, 2 sc in next sc*, rep 6 times. (96 sts)

**Rnd 17:** *Sc 15, 2 sc in next sc*, rep 6 times. (102 sts)

**Rnd 18:** *Sc 16, 2 sc in next sc*, rep 6 times. (108 sts)

**Rnd 19:** *Sc 17, 2 sc in next sc*, rep 6 times. (114 sts)

**Rnd 20:** *Sc 18, 2 sc in next sc*, rep 6 times. (120 sts)

**Rnd 21:** *Sc 19, 2 sc in next sc*, rep 6 times. (126 sts)

**Rnd 22:** *Sc 20, 2 sc in next sc*, rep 6 times. (132 sts)

**Rnd 23:** *Sc 21, 2 sc in next sc*, rep 6 times. (138 sts)

**Rnd 24:** *Sc 22, 2 sc in next sc*, rep 6 times. (144 sts)

**Rnds 25–33:** Sc 144.

Sl st 1 and fasten off.

## SHELL BOTTOM

Using H hook and orange yarn, work rnds 1–24 as for top.

**Rnds 25–26:** Sc 144.

Sl st 1 and fasten off, leaving long tail for sewing. Using tapestry needle, sew shell bottom to top three quarters of the way around, stuff and finish sewing seam to close.

## CHEEK

Make 2.

**Rnd 1:** Using H hook and pink yarn, ch 2, 5 sc in second ch from hook.

**Rnd 2:** Sc 2 in every sc around. (10 sts)

Sl st 1 and fasten off, leaving long tail for sewing. Set aside.

## TURTLE HEAD

**Rnd 1:** Using I hook and green yarn, ch 2, 6 sc in second ch from hook.

**Rnd 2:** Sc 2 in every sc around. (12 sts)

**Rnd 3:** *Sc 1, 2 sc in next sc*, rep 6 times. (18 sts)

**Rnd 4:** *Sc 2, 2 sc in next sc*, rep 6 times. (24 sts)

**Rnd 5:** *Sc 3, 2 sc in next sc*, rep 6 times. (30 sts)

**Rnd 6:** *Sc 4, 2 sc in next sc*, rep 6 times. (36 sts)

**Rnds 7–12:** Sc 36.

**Rnd 13:** *Sc 4, dec 1*, rep 6 times. (30 sts)

**Rnd 14:** Sc 30.

Sl st 1 and fasten off, leaving long tail for sewing.

**Work on face:** Insert plastic eyes with safety backings. Embroider mouth. Sew cheeks in place.

Stuff head and sew to body between rnd 25 of top and rnd 23 of bottom.

## LEG

Make 4.

**Rnd 1:** Using I hook and green yarn, ch 2, 5 sc in second ch from hook. (5 sts)

**Rnd 2:** Sc 2 in every sc around. (10 sts)

**Rnd 3:** *Sc 2, 2 sc in next sc*, rep 5 times. (15 sts)

**Rnds 4–8:** Sc 15.

Sl st 1 and fasten off, leaving long tail for sewing. Stuff a little, sew open end closed, and sew legs to shell where top and bottom of shell meet (2 on each side).

## TAIL

Using I hook and green yarn, loosely ch 7.

Starting in second ch from hook, sl st 1, 1 sc, 1 hdc, 3 dc.

Fasten off and sew to shell at back end.

# Tree Stump Floor Cushion

*I think this tree stump is my favorite project in this book, and it's the one that I'm keeping for myself. It's going to go either in our living room or my bedroom. It would look great in my "crocheting room," but my husband took over and I'm back in my "office"—also known as the couch! I love this cushion and I think it'll look cute in any room of the house. What room are you planning to crochet it for?*

**FINISHED SIZE: APPROX 6" TALL x 13" IN DIAMETER**

## MATERIALS

Worsted-weight yarn in tan (approx 328 yds), brown (approx 220 yds), and green (approx 35 yds)

Size J-10 (6 mm) crochet hook

9 mm plastic eyes with safety backings

Black embroidery floss and embroidery needle

Tapestry needle

Fiberfill or stuffing of your choice

## CUSHION

**Rnd 1:** Using tan yarn, ch 3, 10 hdc in third ch from hook.

**Rnd 2:** Hdc 2 in every hdc around. (20 sts)

**Rnd 3:** Sc 20.

**Rnd 4:** Hdc 2 in every sc around. (40 sts)

**Rnd 5:** Sc 40.

**Rnd 6:** *Hdc 1, 2 hdc in next sc*, rep 20 times. (60 sts)

**Rnd 7:** Sc 60.

**Rnds 8 and 9:** Hdc 60.

**Rnd 10:** *Sc 2, 2 sc in next hdc*, rep 20 times. (80 sts)

**Rnds 11 and 12:** Hdc 80.

**Rnd 13:** *Sc 3, 2 sc in next hdc*, rep 20 times. (100 sts)

**Rnds 14 and 15:** Hdc 100.

**Rnd 16:** *Sc 4, 2 sc in next hdc*. (120 sts)

**Rnds 17 and 18:** Hdc 120.

**Rnd 19:** *Sc 5, 2 sc in next hdc*, rep 20 times. (140 sts)

**Rnds 20 and 21:** Hdc 140.

Change to brown yarn.

**Rnd 22:** Sc 140 through back loops only (see page 72).

**Rnd 23:** *Sc 6, 2 sc in next sc*, rep 20 times. (160 sts)

**Rnds 24–39:** Sc 160.

Change to tan yarn.

**Rnd 40:** Sc 160 through back loops only.

**Rnd 41:** *Sc 6, sc dec 1*, rep 20 times. (140 sts)

**Rnd 42:** Hdc 140.

**Rnd 43:** *Sc 5, sc dec 1*, rep 20 times. (120 sts)

**Rnds 44 and 45:** Hdc 120.

**Rnd 46:** *Sc 4, sc dec 1*, rep 20 times. (100 sts)

**Rnds 47 and 48:** Hdc 100.

**Rnd 49:** *Sc 3, sc dec 1*, rep 20 times. (80 sts)

**Rnds 50 and 51:** Hdc 80.

**Rnd 52:** *Sc 2, sc dec 1*, rep 20 times. (60 sts)

**Rnds 53 and 54:** Hdc 60.

**Rnd 55:** Sc 60.

**Rnd 56:** *Hdc 1, hdc dec 1*, rep 20 times. (40 sts)

**Rnd 57:** Sc 40.

Stuff almost to top.

**Rnd 58:** Sc dec 10 times. (20 sts)

**Rnd 59:** Hdc 20.

**Rnd 60:** Sc dec 10 times. (10 sts)

Finish stuffing.

**Rnd 61:** Sc dec 5 times. (5 sts)

Fasten off, leaving long tail to close up 5-st hole.

## BRANCH

**Rnd 1:** Using brown yarn, ch 2, 5 sc in second ch from hook.

**Rnd 2:** Sc 5.

**Rnd 3:** Sc 2 in every sc around. (10 sts)

**Rnd 4:** Sc 10.

**Rnd 5:** *Sc 1, 2 sc in next sc*, rep 5 times. (15 sts)

**Rnd 6:** Sc 15.

**Rnd 7:** *Sc 2, 2 sc in next sc*, rep 5 times. (20 sts)

**Rnd 8:** Sc 20.

**Rnd 9:** *Sc 3, 2 sc in next sc*, rep 5 times. (25 sts)

**Rnds 10–13:** Sc 25.

Sl st 1 and fasten off, leaving long tail for sewing. Stuff and use tapestry needle to sew to tree trunk in middle of brown area.

## WORM

Worm is made in sections.

### Head

**Rnd 1:** Using green yarn, ch 2, 5 sc in second ch from hook.

**Rnd 2:** Sc 2 in every sc around. (10 sts)

**Rnd 3:** *Sc 1, 2 sc in next sc*, rep 5 times. (15 sts)

**Rnd 4:** *Sc 2, 2 sc in next sc*, rep 5 times. (20 sts)

**Rnds 5–10:** Sc 20.

**Rnd 11:** *Sc 2, dec 1*, rep 5 times. (15 sts)

**Work on face:** Attach plastic eyes with safety backings. Embroider smile.

**Rnd 12:** *Sc 1, dec 1*, rep 5 times. (10 sts)

Stuff head.

**Rnd 13:** Dec 5 times. (5 sts)

Fasten off.

### Antenna

Make 2.

Join yarn on side of head, ch 4. Fasten off.

### Body

Make 3 balls.

**Rnd 1:** Using green yarn, ch 2, 5 sc in second ch from hook.

**Rnd 2:** Sc 2 in every sc around. (10 sts)

**Rnds 3 and 4:** Sc 10.

**Rnd 5:** Dec 5 times. (5 sts)

Sl st 1 and fasten off, leaving long tail to close 5-st hole. Stuff and stitch hole closed. Referring to photo on page 62, sew three balls tog, then sew to side of worm head below eyes. Sew worm to branch.

# Toys and Books Basket

*Oli and Martina love to read, which is great. But what's not great is that whenever they bring what they're reading downstairs, they forget to put them back in their bookcases. Consequentially, there are books on every horizontal surface in the kitchen, living room, and dining room!*

*I figured it was time to do something about this mess, so I made a basket and added the mushroom in the middle. This way they can put their books inside and take it upstairs to put everything back in its place. You could also use it for magazines or toys, or my favorite, lots of yarn!*

**FINISHED SIZE: APPROX 9" TALL x 14" IN DIAMETER**

## MATERIALS

Worsted-weight yarn in white (approx 40 yds) and red (approx 30 yds)

Chunky-weight yarn in brown (approx 405 yds) and green (approx 15 yds) 5

Size H-8 (5 mm) crochet hook

Size K-10½ (6.5 mm) crochet hook

Tapestry needle

Fiberfill or stuffing of your choice

## BASKET

**Rnd 1:** Using K hook and brown yarn, ch 3, 10 hdc in third ch from hook.

**Rnd 2:** Hdc 2 in every hdc around. (20 sts)

**Rnd 3:** Sc 20.

**Rnd 4:** Hdc 2 in every sc around. (40 sts)

**Rnd 5:** Sc 40.

**Rnd 6:** *Hdc 1, 2 hdc in next sc*, rep 20 times. (60 sts)

**Rnd 7:** Sc 60.

**Rnds 8 and 9:** Hdc 60.

**Rnd 10:** *Sc 2, 2 sc in next hdc*, rep 20 times. (80 sts)

**Rnds 11 and 12:** Hdc 80.

**Rnd 13:** *Sc 3, 2 sc in next hdc*, rep 20 times. (100 sts)

**Rnds 14 and 15:** Hdc 100.

**Rnd 16:** *Sc 4, 2 sc in next hdc*. (120 sts)

**Rnds 17 and 18:** Hdc 120.

**Rnd 19:** *Sc 5, 2 sc in next hdc*, rep 20 times. (140 sts)

**Rnds 20 and 21:** Hdc 140.

**Rnd 22:** Sc 140 through back loops only (see page 72).

**Rnds 23–58:** Sc 140.

Sl st 1 and fasten off.

*Handle support sewn
to inside of basket*

## HANDLE

Make 2.

Using K hook and green yarn, loosely ch 31, leaving long tail for sewing.

**Row 1:** Sc 30 starting in second ch from hook, turn.

**Rows 2 and 3:** Ch 1, 30 sc, turn.

Fasten off, leaving long tail for sewing. Using tapestry needle, sew about 1" of each end of handle to outside of basket at top, with ends about 1" apart. Repeat on opposite side for second handle.

## HANDLE SUPPORT

Make 2. These will make the area where the handles are attached a bit sturdier.

Using K hook and brown yarn, loosely ch 11.

**Row 1:** Sc 10 starting in second ch from hook, turn.

**Rows 2–20:** Ch 1, 10 sc, turn.

Fasten off. On inside of basket, align long edge of rectangle with top edge of basket where handle is attached. Sew all around.

Use brown yarn to embroider an X on each handle end.

## MUSHROOM

Mushroom is made in sections.

### Cap

**Rnd 1:** Using H hook and red yarn, ch 2, 6 sc in second ch from hook.

**Rnd 2:** Sc 2 in each sc around. (12 sts)

**Rnd 3:** *Sc 1, 2 sc in next sc*, rep 6 times. (18 sts)

**Rnd 4:** *Sc 2, 2 sc in next sc*, rep 6 times. (24 sts)

**Rnd 5:** *Sc 3, 2 sc in next sc*, rep 6 times. (30 sts)

**Rnds 6 and 7:** Sc 30.

**Rnd 8:** *Sc 4, 2 sc in next sc*, rep 6 times. (36 sts)

**Rnds 9 and 10:** Sc 36.

**Rnd 11:** *Sc 5, 2 sc in next sc*, rep 6 times. (42 sts)

**Rnds 12 and 13:** Sc 42.

**Rnd 14:** *Sc 6, 2 sc in next sc*, rep 6 times. (48 sts)

**Rnds 15 and 16:** Sc 48.

**Rnd 17:** *Sc 7, 2 sc in next sc*, rep 6 times. (54 sts)

**Rnds 18 and 19:** Sc 54.

**Rnd 20:** *Sc 8, 2 sc in next sc*, rep 6 times. (60 sts)

**Rnd 21:** *Sc 9, 2 sc in next sc*, rep 6 times. (66 sts)

**Rnds 22 and 23:** Sc 66.

Fasten off, leaving long tail for sewing.

## Spot

Make 5, or whatever number you desire.

**Rnd 1:** Using H hook and white yarn, ch 2, 6 sc in second ch from hook.

**Rnd 2:** Sc 2 in each sc around. (12 sts)

**Rnd 3:** *Sc 1, 2 sc in next sc*, rep 6 times. (18 sts)

Sl st 1 and fasten off, leaving long tail for sewing. Sew to mushroom cap.

## Stem

**Rnd 1:** Using H hook and white yarn, ch 2, 6 sc in second ch from hook.

**Rnd 2:** Sc 2 in each sc around. (12 sts)

**Rnd 3:** *Sc 1, 2 sc in next sc*, rep 6 times. (18 sts)

**Rnd 4:** *Sc 2, 2 sc in next sc*, rep 6 times. (24 sts)

**Rnd 5:** *Sc 3, 2 sc in next sc*, rep 6 times. (30 sts)

**Rnd 6:** Through back loops only, 30 sc.

**Rnds 7–13:** Sc 30.

**Rnd 14:** *Sc 4, 2 sc in next sc*, rep 6 times. (36 sts)

**Rnd 15:** *Sc 5, 2 sc in next sc*, rep 6 times. (42 sts)

**Rnd 16:** *Sc 6, 2 sc in next sc*, rep 6 times. (48 sts)

**Rnd 17:** *Sc 7, 2 sc in next sc*, rep 6 times. (54 sts)

**Rnd 18:** *Sc 8, 2 sc in next sc*, rep 6 times. (60 sts)

**Rnd 19:** Sc 60.

Sl st 1 and fasten off, leaving long tail for sewing. Sew top of stem to rnd 21 on underside of cap approx three quarters of the way around, stuff mushroom top and stem, and finish sewing. Sew rnd 5 of stem to center bottom of basket.

*The little mushroom keeps the books from falling over.*

# General Guidelines

Simple crochet skills are all you need to make these delightful amigurumi accessories.

## YARN

The projects in this book are crocheted using worsted-weight yarn and a size G-6 (4 mm), an H-8 (5 mm), or a J-10 (6 mm) hook, and occasionally a size I-9 (5.5 mm) or K-10½ (6.5 mm) hook with chunky-weight yarn.

I used acrylic yarn for these projects because pillows, rugs, and cushions can become very dirty, and acrylic seems to hold up better than other fibers when put in the washing machine. A list of the yarn I used for the samples in this book can be found on page 77, but it doesn't really matter which brand you use. Choose colors similar to mine, or be creative and come up with your own color combinations!

## GAUGE, TENSION, AND HOOK SIZES

The measurements given for each project are approximate and based on the way I crochet. I crochet pretty tightly, and with a J hook and worsted-weight yarn, my gauge is as follows:

   35 sc and 7 rounds = 3"-diameter circle

   50 sc and 10 rounds = 4"-diameter circle

The finished size, however, isn't really that important, so don't worry if your gauge is different from mine. Depending on your tension and the yarn you use, your project might end up being a little bit smaller or larger than the ones I made. Changing to a bigger or smaller hook will give you a bigger or smaller project, respectively.

# STITCHES

Simple stitches are used for these amigurumi projects, making them perfect for beginners!

**Chain (ch).** Make a slipknot and place it on the hook. Yarn over the hook, draw the yarn through the slipknot, and let the slipknot slide off the hook. *Yarn over the hook, draw the yarn through the new loop, and let the loop slide off the hook. Repeat from * for the desired number of chain stitches.

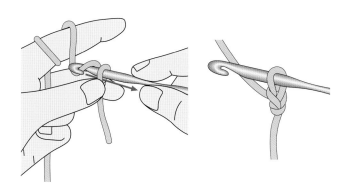

**Slip stitch (sl st).** A slip stitch is used to move across one or more stitches. Insert the hook into the stitch, yarn over the hook, and pull through both loops on the hook at once.

**Single crochet (sc).** *Insert the hook into the chain or stitch indicated, yarn over the hook, and pull through the chain or stitch (two loops on the hook).

Yarn over the hook and pull through the two loops on the hook. Repeat from * for the required number of stitches.

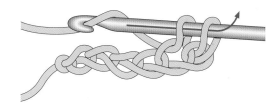

**Single crochet increase.** Work two single crochet stitches into the same stitch.

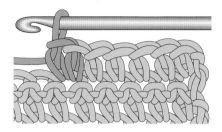

**Single crochet decrease (dec).** (Insert the hook into the next stitch, yarn over, pull up a loop) twice; yarn over and pull through all three loops on the hook.

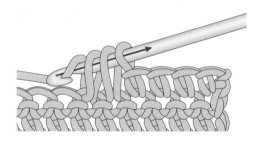

**Half double crochet (hdc).** *Yarn over the hook and insert the hook into the chain or stitch indicated. Yarn over the hook and pull through the stitch (three loops on the hook).

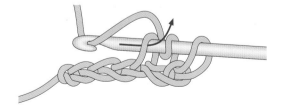

Yarn over the hook and pull through all three loops on the hook. Repeat from * for the required number of stitches.

**Half double crochet increase.** Work two half double crochet stitches into the same stitch.

**Half double crochet decrease (hdc dec).** *Yarn over the hook and insert the hook into the next stitch, yarn over the hook and pull through the stitch (three loops on the hook). Yarn over the hook and insert the hook into the next stitch, yarn over the hook and pull through the stitch. Yarn over the hook and pull through all five loops on the hook.

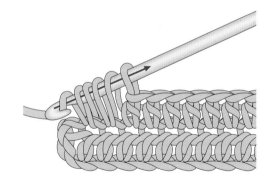

**Double crochet (dc).** *Yarn over the hook and insert the hook into the chain or stitch indicated. Yarn over the hook and pull through the stitch (three loops on the hook); yarn over the hook and pull through two loops on the hook (two loops on the hook).

**Triple crochet (tr).** *Yarn over the hook twice and insert the hook into the chain or stitch indicated. Yarn over the hook and pull through the stitch (four loops on hook). Yarn over the hook and pull through two loops on the hook (three loops remain on the hook).

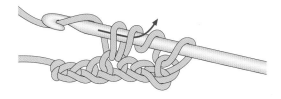

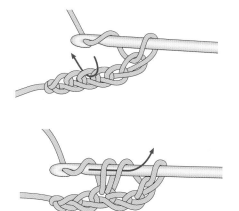

(Yarn over the hook and pull through two loops on the hook) twice (one loop remains on the hook). Repeat from * for the required number of stitches.

Yarn over the hook and pull through the remaining two loops on the hook (one loop on the hook). Repeat from * for the required number of stitches.

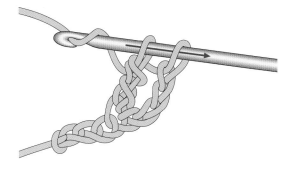

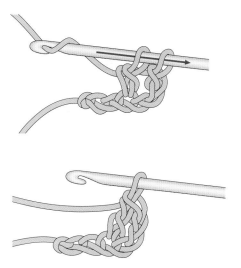

## WORKING IN CHAIN LOOPS

When crocheting the first row into the beginning chain, the first row of stitches is generally worked into one or both loops on the right side of the chain.

Crocheting into top loop

Crocheting into both loops

For some projects, the first row of stitches is worked in the "bump" on the wrong side of the chain.

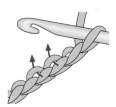

## WORKING IN STITCH LOOPS

The majority of the stitches are worked in both loops of the stitches from the previous row. There are a few projects where you will work into the back loop or the front loop of the stitch.

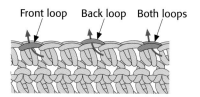

Front loop   Back loop   Both loops

## CROCHETING IN THE ROUND

When crocheting in the round, I crochet around and around, forming a continuous spiral without joining rounds. To keep track of where the rounds begin and end, you can mark the end or beginning of a round with a safety pin, stitch marker, or little piece of different-colored yarn pulled through one of the stitches. At the end of the last round, slip stitch in the first single crochet of the previous round and fasten off the yarn.

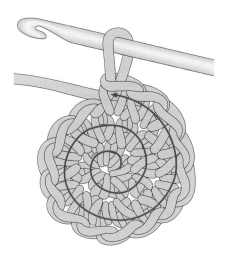

## CHANGING YARN COLORS

Some projects require alternating two colors in the body. To do this, work the last stitch of a round until one step remains in the stitch; then work the last step with the new color and continue the round in the new color. Continue to the end of the round and change color in the same manner.

## ADDING FACES

The patterns for muzzles and any other pieces to be cut from felt are included with each project. Cut the felt pieces with sharp scissors to get nice, smooth edges. Using embroidery floss and a needle, I use simple stitches to "draw" the faces on the felt before attaching the felt pieces to the accessories. Sew pieces of felt on with a sharp needle and matching sewing thread. Use a very small running stitch close to the edge of the piece.

### Mouths

For a simple mouth, bring the needle out at point A and insert the needle at point B, leaving a loose strand of floss to form the mouth. Once you're happy with the shape of the mouth, bring the needle out again at point C, cross over the loose strand of floss, and insert the needle at point D to make a tiny stitch. Secure the ends on the wrong side.

### Noses and Eyes

To satin stitch features, bring the needle out through point A, insert at point B, and repeat, following the shape you want for the nose or eyes and making sure to work the stitches really close together. Secure the ends on the wrong side.

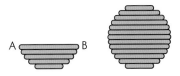

Another option for embroidering a nose is to work from a center point upward (like for the Owl Pillow on page 9). Bring the needle up from underneath at point A; insert the needle at point B. Bring the needle up at point C, very close to point A. Insert the needle back into point B. Continue working stitches close to each other to create a triangle, making sure to always insert the needle back into point B. When you're satisfied with the triangle, make two long stitches across the top of the nose to help define it.

## STUFFING

I always use polyester fiberfill stuffing because it's nonallergenic, won't bunch up, and it's washable, which is always good when you're making things that may need to be washed often! If you do wash these items, make sure you follow the care instructions on the yarn label.

## ADDING THE EXTREMITIES

I always use a tapestry needle and the same color of yarn as the pieces (or at least one of the pieces) that I want to sew together. When joining pieces, make sure they are securely attached so that little fingers can't pull them off.

On some projects, the opening of the animal extremities will remain open for sewing onto the body; the instructions will tell you when to leave them open. Position the limb on the body and sew all around it, going through the front stitches of both the limb and the body.

On other projects, the opening of the extremities will be sewn closed before being attached to the body. To do this, pinch the opening closed, line up the stitches of one side with the other side, and sew through the front loop of one side and the back loop of the other side. Position the piece where you want it on the body and sew it in place.

## WHIPSTITCH

This easy stitch is used in some of the projects to sew pieces together.

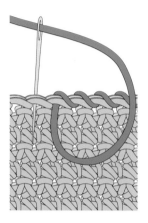

## ADDING ZIPPERS

Sewing zippers is a lot easier than it seems! With the right side of the project facing you, align the zipper (from the inside of the project) with the project's opening. Make sure the zipper pull is touching one of the ends of the project's opening so you won't have a hole in the corner. Close the zipper and baste it in place with a sewing needle and contrasting-color sewing thread (so it's easier to see). Once you're done, sew it in place with a tapestry needle and yarn to match the project. Sew one side, and then open the zipper and sew the other side. Presto!

Don't worry if your zipper is longer than the opening. You can either leave the extra part inside the floor cushion or trim it off, making sure you secure the end with several tight stitches.

## WEAVING IN ENDS

When you bind off your work, make sure to leave a tail 4" long so that you'll be able to hide it in the back of your work. Using a tapestry needle and working on the wrong side of the project, insert the needle into the bottom row of stitches, sliding it behind the two loops of each stitch until you have a little piece left. The shorter the piece, the better, so that you won't have to cut it with scissors and risk cutting your just-finished work!

# Abbreviations and Glossary

|  |  |
|---|---|
| * | repeat directions between * and * as many times as indicated |
| approx | approximately |
| ch | chain |
| cont | continue |
| dc | double crochet |
| dec | single crochet 2 stitches together (see page 70) |
| hdc | half double crochet |
| hdc dec | half double crochet 2 stitches together (see page 70) |
| mm | millimeter(s) |
| patt(s) | pattern(s) |
| rep | repeat |
| rnd(s) | round(s) |
| RS | right side |
| sc | single crochet |
| sk | skip |
| sl st | slip stitch |
| sp | space |
| st(s) | stitch(es) |
| tog | together |
| tr | triple crochet |
| WS | wrong side |
| yd(s) | yard(s) |

# Helpful Information

## STANDARD YARN WEIGHTS

| Yarn-Weight Symbol and Category Name | 1 Super Fine | 2 Fine | 3 Light | 4 Medium | 5 Bulky | 6 Super Bulky |
|---|---|---|---|---|---|---|
| Types of Yarn in Category | Sock, Fingering, Baby | Sport, Baby | DK, Light Worsted | Worsted, Afghan, Aran | Chunky, Craft, Rug | Bulky, Roving |
| Crochet Gauge* Range in Single Crochet to 4" | 21 to 32 sts | 16 to 20 sts | 12 to 17 sts | 11 to 14 sts | 8 to 11 sts | 5 to 9 sts |
| Recommended Hook in Metric Size Range | 2.25 to 3.5 mm | 3.5 to 4.5 mm | 4.5 to 5.5 mm | 5.5 to 6.5 mm | 6.5 to 9 mm | 9 mm and larger |
| Recommended Hook in US Size Range | B-1 to E-4 | E-4 to 7 | 7 to I-9 | I-9 to K-10½ | K-10½ to M-13 | M-13 and larger |

*These are guidelines only. The above reflect the most commonly used gauges and needle or hook sizes for specific yarn categories.*

## METRIC CONVERSIONS

Yards x .91 = meters
Meters x 1.09 = yards
Ounces x 28.35 = grams
Grams x .035 = ounces

## CROCHET HOOK SIZES

| Millimeter | US Size* |
|------------|----------|
| 2.25 mm | B-1 |
| 2.75 mm | C-2 |
| 3.25 mm | D-3 |
| 3.5 mm | E-4 |
| 3.75 mm | F-5 |
| 4 mm | G-6 |
| 4.5 mm | 7 |
| 5 mm | H-8 |
| 5.5 mm | I-9 |
| 6 mm | J-10 |
| 6.5 mm | K-10½ |
| 8 mm | L-11 |
| 9 mm | M/N-13 |

*Letter or number may vary.
Rely on the millimeter sizing.

# Resources

## YARN

**Red Heart Yarn**
www.redheart.com

- *Super Saver Classic*
- *With Love*
- *Super Saver Chunky*

## SAFETY EYES

I used safety eyes in four of the projects in this book and used felt in the rest, but you can always use plastic eyes if you like them better. However, please do not give an item with plastic eyes (or buttons) to a child younger than three years old unless they are being supervised at all times while playing with it. Your local craft store probably carries safety eyes. If you can't find them locally, visit www.sunshinecrafts.com; search for "eyes." They ship them fast. If you want fun, colorful eyes, check out www.suncatchereyes.net.

## ZIPPERS

Zippers can be found at most craft and sewing stores. But you can also find colorful ones in this Etsy shop: www.kandcsupplies.etsy.com.

# Acknowledgments

Thank you so much, Red Heart, for supplying all the yarn for this book. Getting the box full of yarn was better than Christmas morning!

Thank you very much, Ursula (you are so nice and so patient with me; I know I'm not the best at turning everything in on time!), and everybody at Martingale for always being so nice and making the books so beautiful!